Appalachia:
a Meditation

Appalachia:
a Meditation

Albert J. Fritsch, S.J.
photographs by Warren E. Brunner

❀ Loyola University Press
Chicago 60657

© 1986 Appalachia—Science in the
  Public Interest
All rights reserved
Printed in the United States of America

Loyola University Press
3441 North Ashland Avenue
Chicago, Illinois 60657

Design by J. L. Boden Trela

Excerpt(s) from THE JERUSALEM BIBLE,
copyright © 1966 by Darton, Longman &
Todd, Ltd. and Doubleday & Company, Inc.
Reprinted by permission of the Publisher.

Library of Congress Cataloging-in-
  Publication Data
Fritsch, Albert J.
  Appalachia: a meditation
  1. Appalachian Region—Description and
travel—Views.   2. Meditations.   I. Brunner,
Warren E.   II. Title
F106.F75   1986   974   86-10457
ISBN 0-8294-0536-4

Contents

vii   **Preface**

1   **Winter**

41   **Spring**

81   **Summer**

121   **Autumn**

Preface

The theme of our book is Appalachia, its land and people. We are convinced that our land has certain qualities which reflect its Creator. However, these qualities are not readily apparent except to those who come in tune with the land—the ones who work it, play on it, live on it, and become like it. Gradually the qualities will become apparent to those who take the time to find them, either in the land itself or in its inhabitants. If we are drawn to Appalachia and its culture in any way, we can make the land itself our teacher. It is truly a humbling experience, but also an opportunity to find what we lack, to renew ourselves, and to be drawn closer to each other and to God.

We present some typical photos of Appalachia here. They are black-and-white glimpses of our portion of America. We have identified seventy-two qualities or characteristics of our land and people and have selected photographs to illustrate them. Since many Appalachian people are in tune with the land, they are keenly aware of the weather and the seasons. And so our selections have been

Acknowledgments

organized according to the four seasons, beginning with winter and ending with autumn. We conceived our little book as a spiritual journey through the Appalachian year, with sadness and joy each in its proper season.

Acknowledgments

We first want to thank the many Appalachian people who allowed us to photograph them and their environment. We took away some of their precious privacy, but we hope that the sharing with others will be its own reward. We also want to thank the following people who helped with the work of assembling this book: Chris Fritsch and Paul Korterud who helped select the photos, Mary Davis for editing the subscripts, Chris Klug for helping with the Scriptural selections, John O'Neill for technical work, and Marie Cirillo for inspiration.

Winter

Winter

From the beginning till now the entire creation, as we know, has been groaning in one great act of giving birth . . .

Romans 8:22

Winter has a way of lulling us to sleep. The countryside seems so quiet and motionless. But is there really nothing happening? Geologists tell us otherwise. The earth itself is in a great process of building up and tearing down, of ongoing motion. It is a restless living organism—and it's in a very long process of giving birth. But to what or to whom? Maybe it's giving birth to all of us. We are being born from the earth itself—but we are so close to the process that we don't realize it.

Winter

To you, a thousand years are a single day, a yesterday now over, an hour of the night.

Psalm 90:4

Does time stand still in winter? To those who are snowbound it certainly seems that way. But the days get longer even when winter is in its infancy. The hills themselves take the seasons in stride. They might appear timeless, especially in frozen winter, but one knows that they change—both from natural forces and from human activities. Yes, the silent bell will ring again with the coming of spring.

Winter

This will be your land with the boundaries surrounding it.
                        Numbers 34:12

     Land is different from air. Land can be divided and staked off and bordered with fences. This has its good points and bad points. I can say, "this is my land," and mean that I hold it through a legal title. But what does this do to other people? Do I forbid them the use of it? Do I post "No Trespassing" signs? Fencing may hold the farm animals in, but it may also keep the nut gatherers, berry pickers, wood choppers, and hikers out. "My land" could well be "our land" with many people included. Appalachia is our to-be-shared land.

Winter

Then taking him outside he said, "Look up to the heavens and count the stars if you can. Such will be your descendants," he told him.

Genesis 15:5

      Our people who have moved up North to the cities say they can't see the stars at night. What's it all worth? How can you live without seeing the stars and the moon and the heavens? We can't spend a lot of time gazing upward, and we don't let the stars lead our lives, but they're there all the same. And when we are outside at night, we get lost amid all their beauty. Yet the heavens have a way of helping us find ourselves.

Winter

*Into the sea all the rivers go, and yet
 the sea is never filled,
and still to their goal the rivers go.*

                  Ecclesiastes 1:7

      Nature's forces seem to have made an ongoing commitment to a set pattern, a somewhat predictable way of acting. These forces change the earth by fits and starts, and then so gently that we hardly know they are operating; they carve, shape, mold, and cast the hills and valleys. They move on almost without effort in their seemingly eternal vow of obedience. They draw us in and invite us to harmonize with their rhythms.

Winter

You fixed the earth on its foundations,
    unshakable for ever and ever;
you wrapped it with the deep as with
    a robe,
the waters overtopping the mountains.

                    Psalm 104:5-6

      Nothing is quite so reassuring as a cord of wood for the fireplace and a good tight roof overhead. But is this all? In winter we seem to be isolated by snow, driven into a warm corner by the cold, and drawn to quiet pursuits by the long dark hours. But we find that the sleeping earth tells us something more. We need both water and food to live. We need more than just what we have at hand. We are not autonomous beings, independent of others. Our isolation is short-lived at best, and it's a curse as well. It's good to have close neighbors to help break the cabin fever.

Winter

*Rain came down, floods rose, gales blew
   and hurled themselves
against that house, and it did not fall:
   it was founded on rock.*

Psalm 104:5-6

"And indeed, which of you here, intending to build a tower, would not first sit down and work out the cost to see if he had enough to complete it?"

Luke 14:28

    Did you ever watch builders planning to build a house? They must have it all in their heads before they begin to work. Building a good house demands time, patience, know-how, farsightedness, and brainpower.

  Our own life is like a building. We should plan and think about each step. If we are too impulsive, too quick to judge, too fast to decide, what we hope for will never come about. The mountains teach us to take our time, to avoid the fits and starts. They also seem to plan what they are to become.

Winter

*The people that walked in darkness has
   seen a great light;
on those who live in a land of deep
   shadow
a light has shone.*

Isaiah 9:1

      The earth's colors are dark and subdued. They contrast with flowers and birds. Appalachian people reproduce this contrast with the colorful things they make, or dye, or wear, or place around the homestead. Winter can be a drab time if a person refuses to take nature's invitation to pretty up the place. That is what quiltmakers do. They take the tossed-away things and refashion them into something new. They work with nature to make this a better, more colorful place to live.

Winter

The mountains shiver when they see you . . .
                    Habakkuk 3:10

      God's power affects the hills, the rivers, the valleys. The land and all that is in it also reacts to human activity—that sharing in divine power through technology. The machines we use can transform the earth for better or for worse; they are promise or peril. Much depends on how we use them. When we respect the earth and use our machines carefully, we sense the eager response of the earth itself. We are able to work with the earth as building partners, not as intolerant conquerors.

Winter

*Let the mountains and hills bring
a message of peace for the people.*

Psalm 72:3

    We all seek peace of mind and peace of soul. We look to other people for the way. We look to the land itself, the peaceful hills and hollers, the creeks, the fresh air, birds and trees. We also look to the people who know the land and are in harmony with it. They age and begin to look peaceful like the land itself. They have had their ups and downs. Some of their knocks have been hard ones, but their inner peace shines through.

Winter

*Happy the gentle:
they shall have the earth for their
 heritage.*

Matthew 5:4

    Some people are rough and thoughtless and greedy. Others are kind and mild and neighborly. Sometimes it seems that the rough ones have taken over Appalachia. It's not easy to believe that the gentle ones will really conquer in simple ways. During better moments, however, thoughtful folks know that the gentle are on the right track. They are in tune with the land, for it is gentle. It is their heritage.

Winter

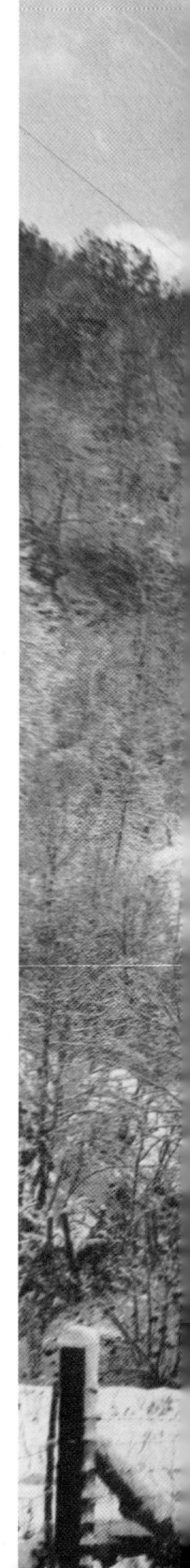

Ever since God created the world his everlasting power and deity—however invisible—have been there for the mind to see in the things he has made.

Romans 1:20

     Another snow falls, blanketing the land and keeping us off the slippery roads. Maybe it's time to collect our thoughts. As children we wondered how each snowflake could have a different pattern. Yet we examine so very few of them. Is all of creation as varied as the snowflakes? There must be hidden treasures of inexhaustible patterns. Who could do all this? Winter gives us a precious opportunity to search for the Lord of the snow and praise him, just as we praise the Lord of spring breezes and summer sunshine.

Winter

*Pride of the heights, shining vault,
so, in a glorious spectacle, the sky
appears.*

                      Ecclesiasticus 43:1

     The land is a gift. So is the sky. So are the trees, the rocks, the silent snow. So are we—both gift and gifted. We are meant for glory, a glory which surpasses that of these majestic hills. Even our blemishes are not lasting; glory will ultimately prevail.

Winter

We are only the earthenware jars which hold this treasure, to make it clear that such an overwhelming power comes from God and not from us.

2 Corinthians 4:7

We come out at sunrise and there it is before us, a fairyland of cut glass on every weed, branch, and human artifact. Touch it and it's gone, so we don't dare reach out. Walk about, and the snowy mass is disturbed. We may try to tiptoe, but even that is too much. We will have to be satisfied with a few handprints, footmarks, and other signs of presence. And we must remember to be gentle at all times.

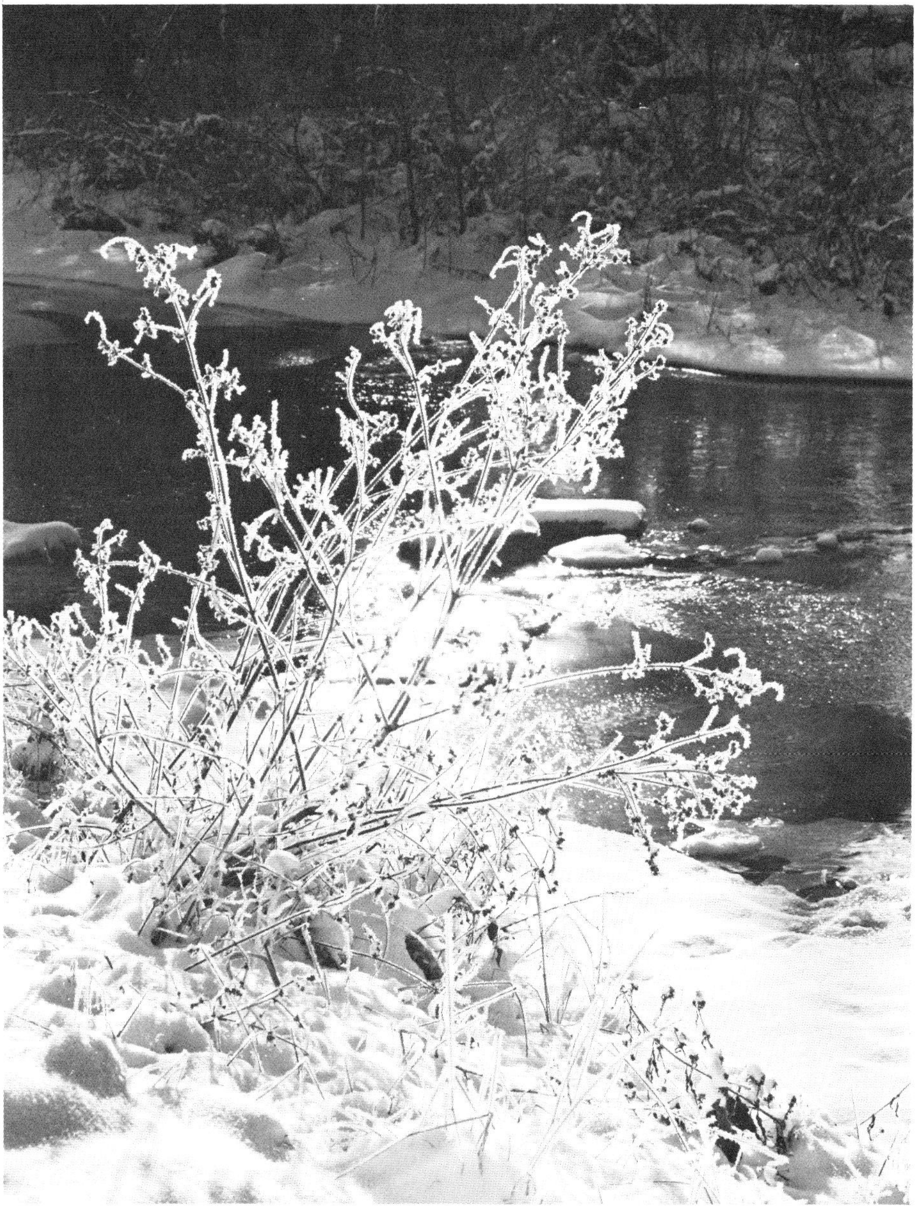

Winter

This is why the country is in mourning,
  and all who live in it pine away,
even the wild animals and the birds
  of heaven;
the fish of the sea themselves are
  perishing.

Hosea 4:3

This is why the land mourns:
  it has been desolated by those who
  skim off the profits;
  it has been stripped away and not
  reclaimed;
  it is used for litter and junk and is not
  cleaned;
  it is poisoned by air pollution and
  water contamination;
  it is made a dump for the hazardous
  wastes of an affluent society;
  it was once fruitful and now is barren;
  it is the victim of our social sin.

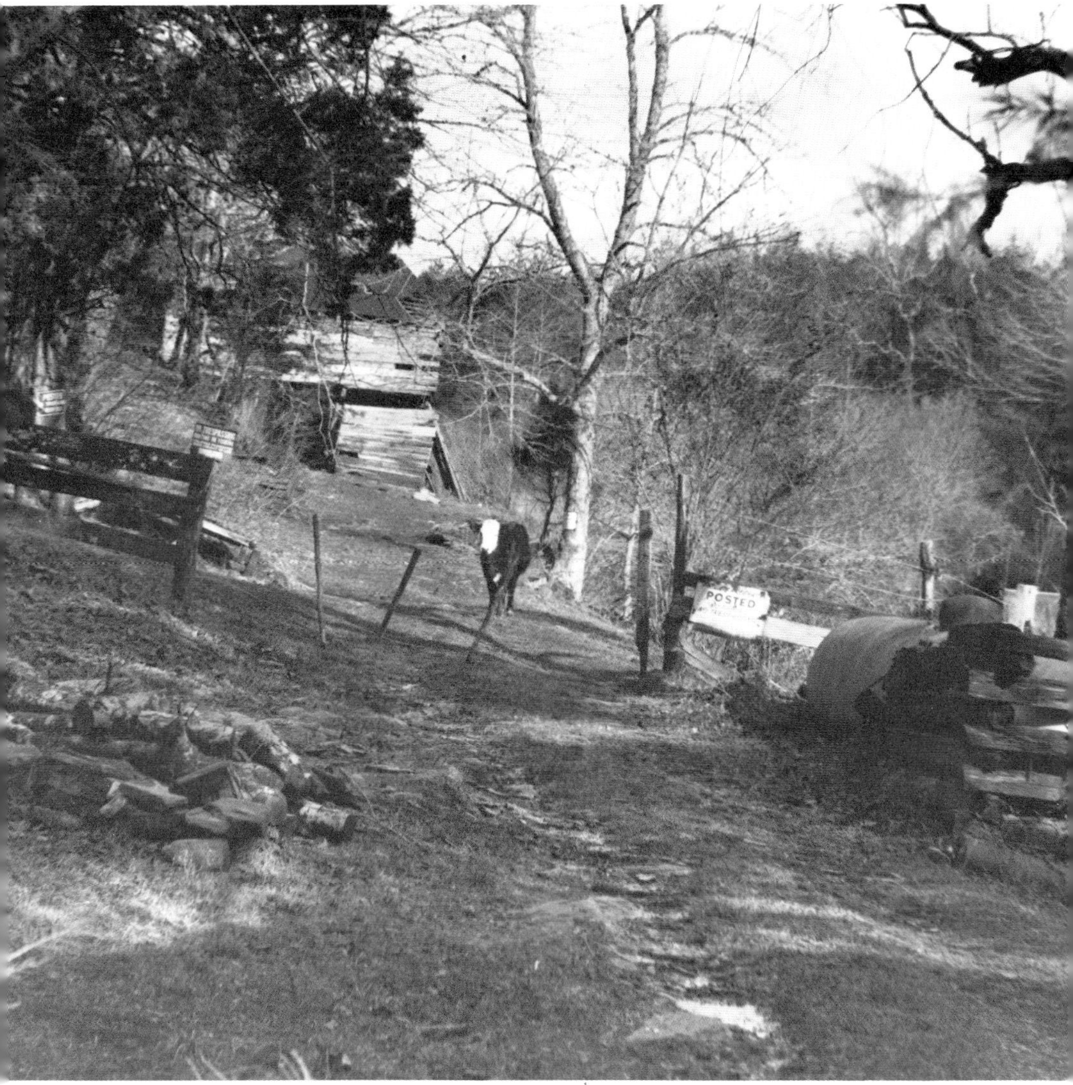
POSTED

Winter

You must not defile the land you inhabit.
                              Numbers 35:34

       Litter is a story in itself. It tells about beauty giving way to ugliness, careless trashing becoming the acceptable thing to do, agencies failing to enforce the law, modern lifestyles generating junk, other people making Appalachia their dumping ground, industry producing non-returnable cans and bottles and leaving the disposal to consumers. The situation threatens a budding recreation industry, and the problem is far from being solved.

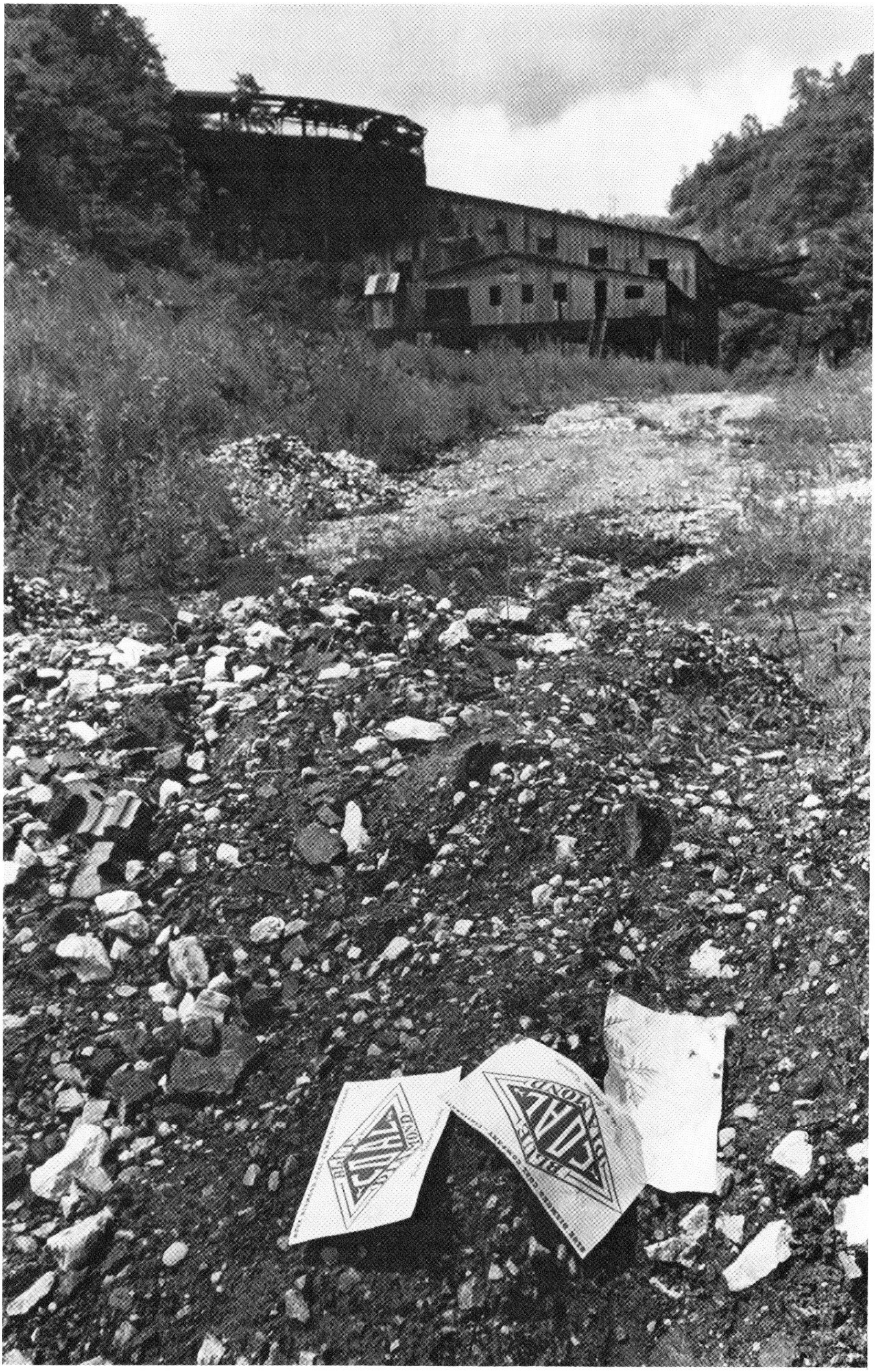
BLUE COAL DIAMOND
BLUE COAL DIAMOND

Winter

Say to the mountains and hills, to the ravines and valleys, "The Lord Yahweh says this: . . . I raise my hand and I swear that the nations around you shall have their own insults to bear."

Ezekiel 36:6-7

"People steal the earth from their children. They do not care. They forget their parents' graves and their children's birthright. They treat their mother, the earth, and their brother, the sky, as things to be bought, plundered, and sold like sheep or bright beads. Their appetites will devour the earth and leave behind only a desert."

Chief Seattle

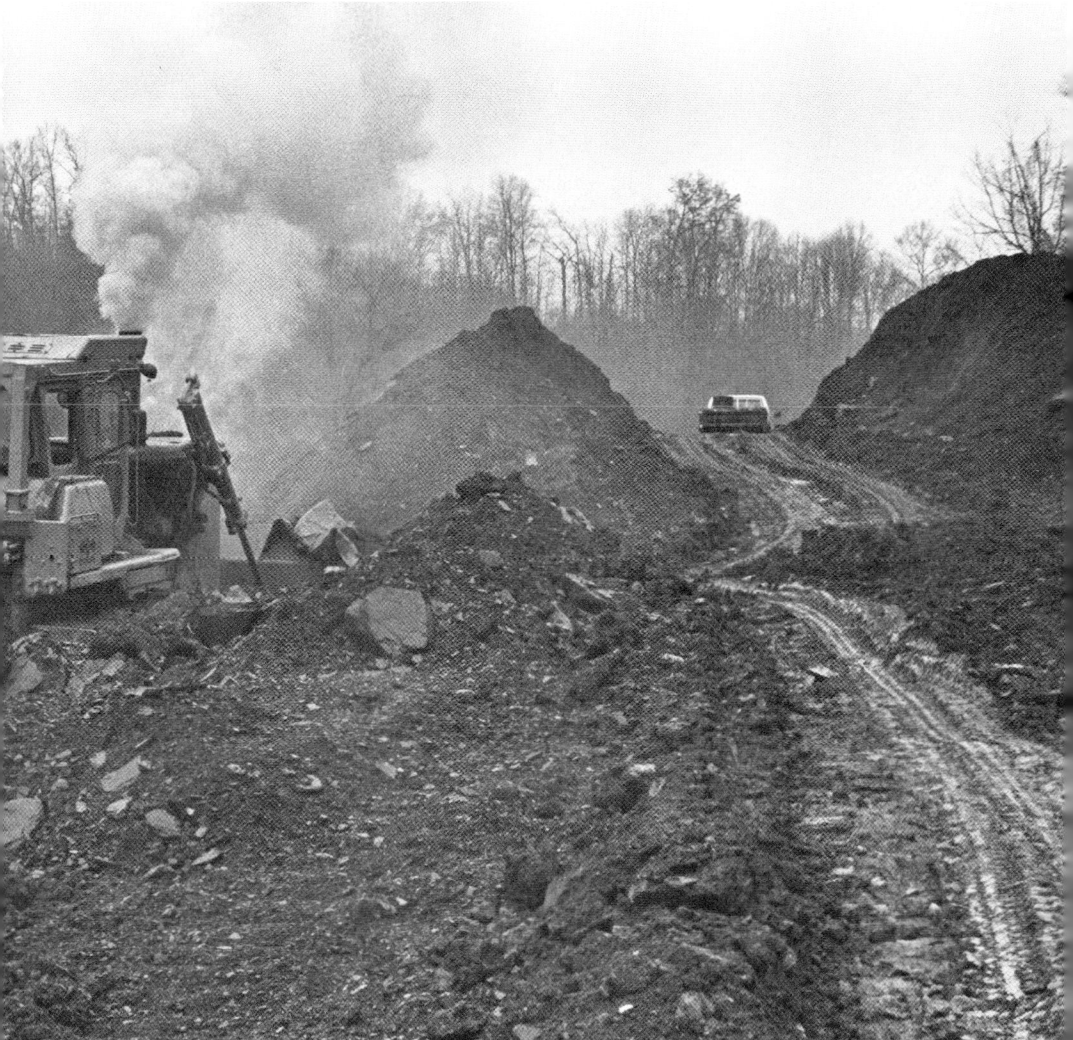

Winter

At that, the veil of the Temple was torn in two from top to bottom; the earth quaked; the rocks were split . . .
                            Matthew 27:51

      The earth does not like to be crucified. To wash away its life is to nail it, scourge it, jeer at it. And the earth itself cries out to heaven. What have we done? What have we done? Can there be new life after this?

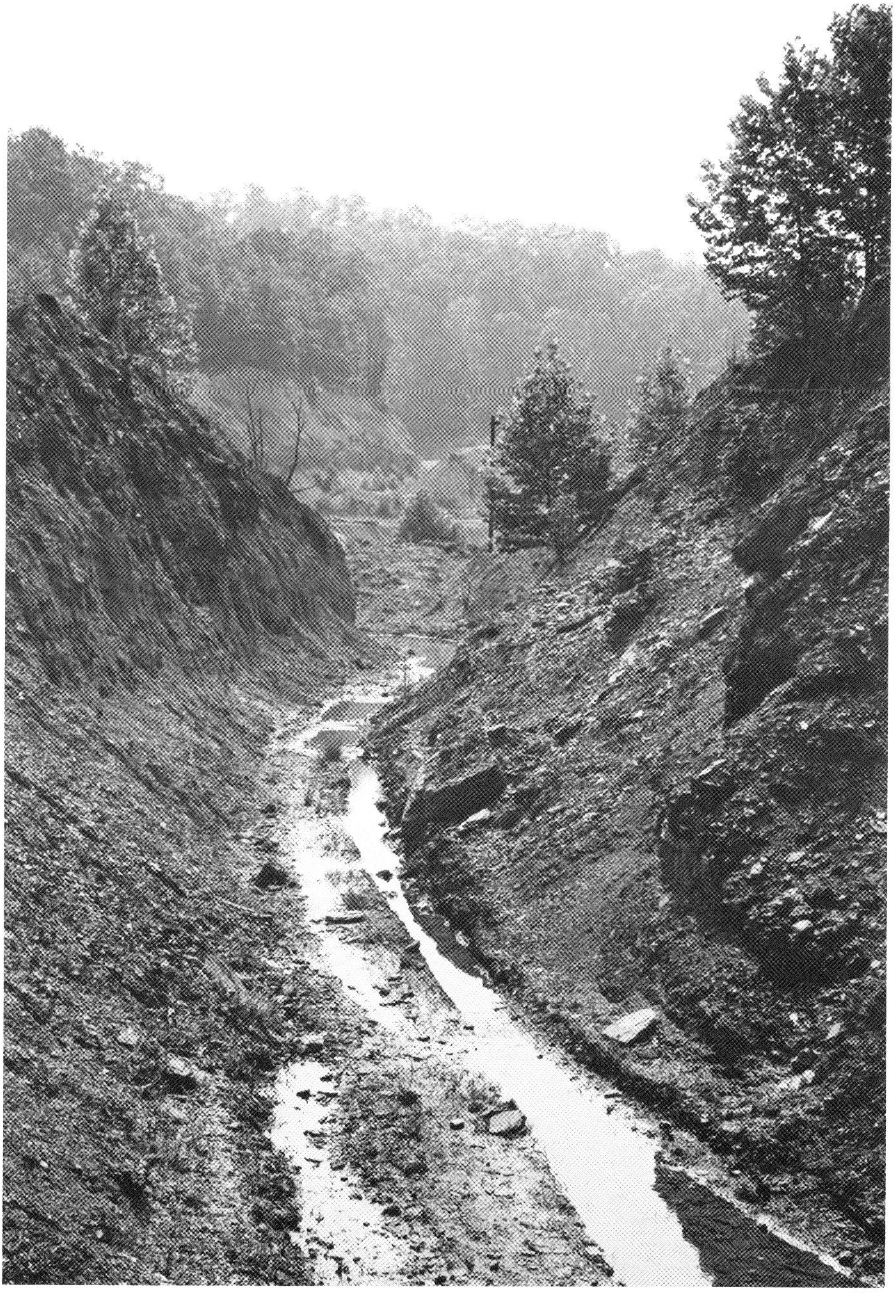

Winter

*Our inheritance has passed to aliens,
our homes to barbarians.*
>   Lamentations 5:2

Who owns this land now? Who controls the destinies of all the people? Who has washed away the smooth clay paths and made rocky roads for people? Who has burdened the footsteps of the elderly and tripped the young at play? Oh, who has saddened a happy land? Have not distant holders of Broadform Deed and mineral rights to wooded dale and sacred hills wrought these deeds? Oh, will these faceless few now fence our ancient trails?

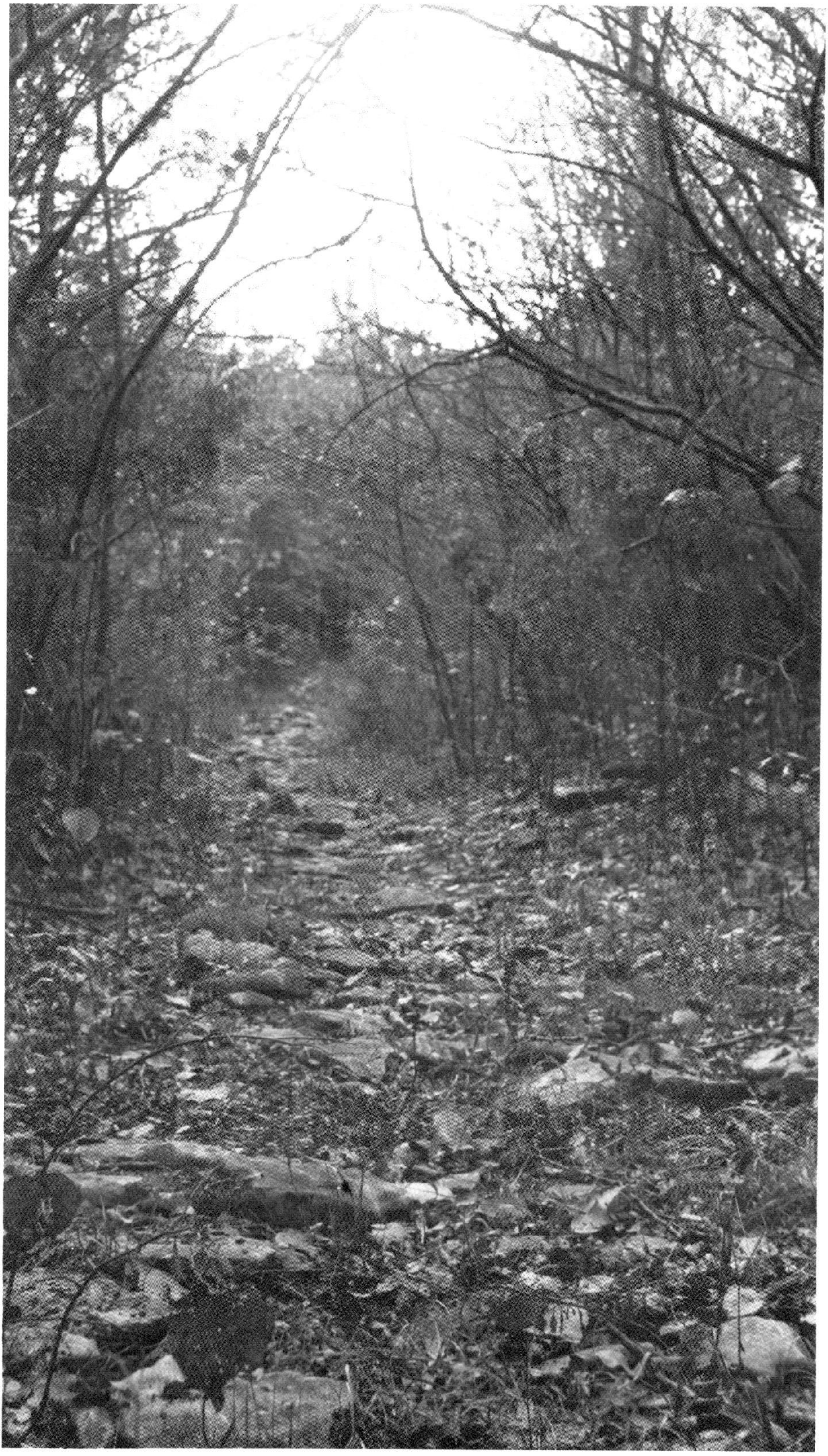

Spring

Spring

*For see, winter is past,
   the rains are over and gone.
The flowers appear on the earth.
The season of glad songs has come,
   the cooing of the turtledove is heard
   in our land.*

   Song of Songs 2:11-12

Winter has been much too long in passing. When you are young, the seasons take a long time to change. When you are fifty or seventy, they go faster. The children want to get outside and play, and we have to understand their restlessness. We also know why they are so happy, why they jump about, and why the schoolyard sounds are more shrill. Children, like all the rest of creation, are just coming alive again.

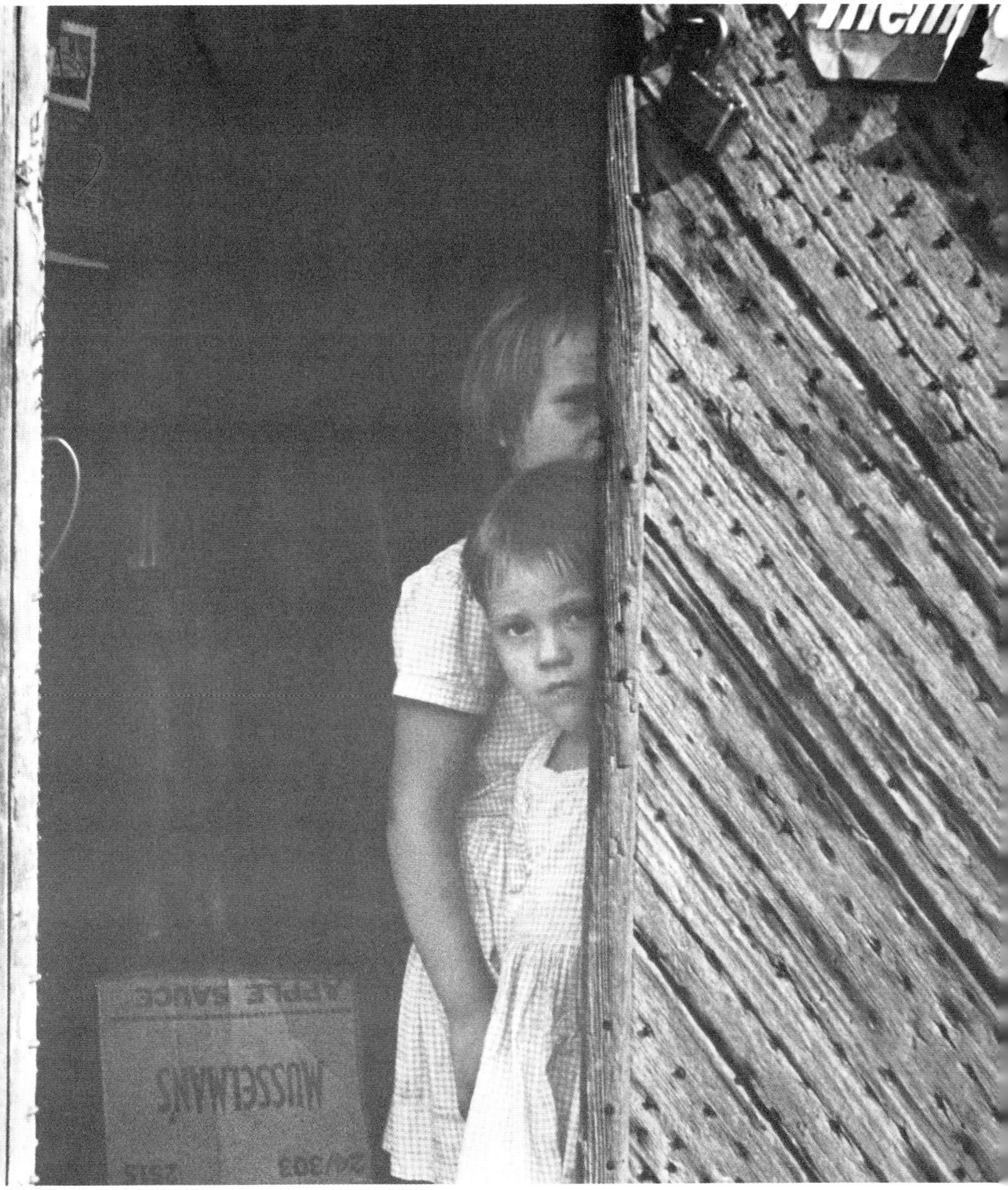
APPLE SAUCE
MUSSELMAN'S
24/303

Spring

*The Spirit of the Lord has been given to
 me,
for he has anointed me.
He has sent me to bring the good news to
 the poor,
to proclaim liberty to captives
and to the blind new sight,
to set the downtrodden free,
to proclaim the Lord's year of favor.*

Luke 4:18-19

From dust to dust and something more. We are free beings. And through chalkdust we become freer still. We learn to read and write, to count and spell. We use books to open up new worlds of ideas and hopes and dreams. And through them we can help others know that they are free as well. And when people break loose and take on their own freedom in imperfect ways, we can surely say, "This is good news!"

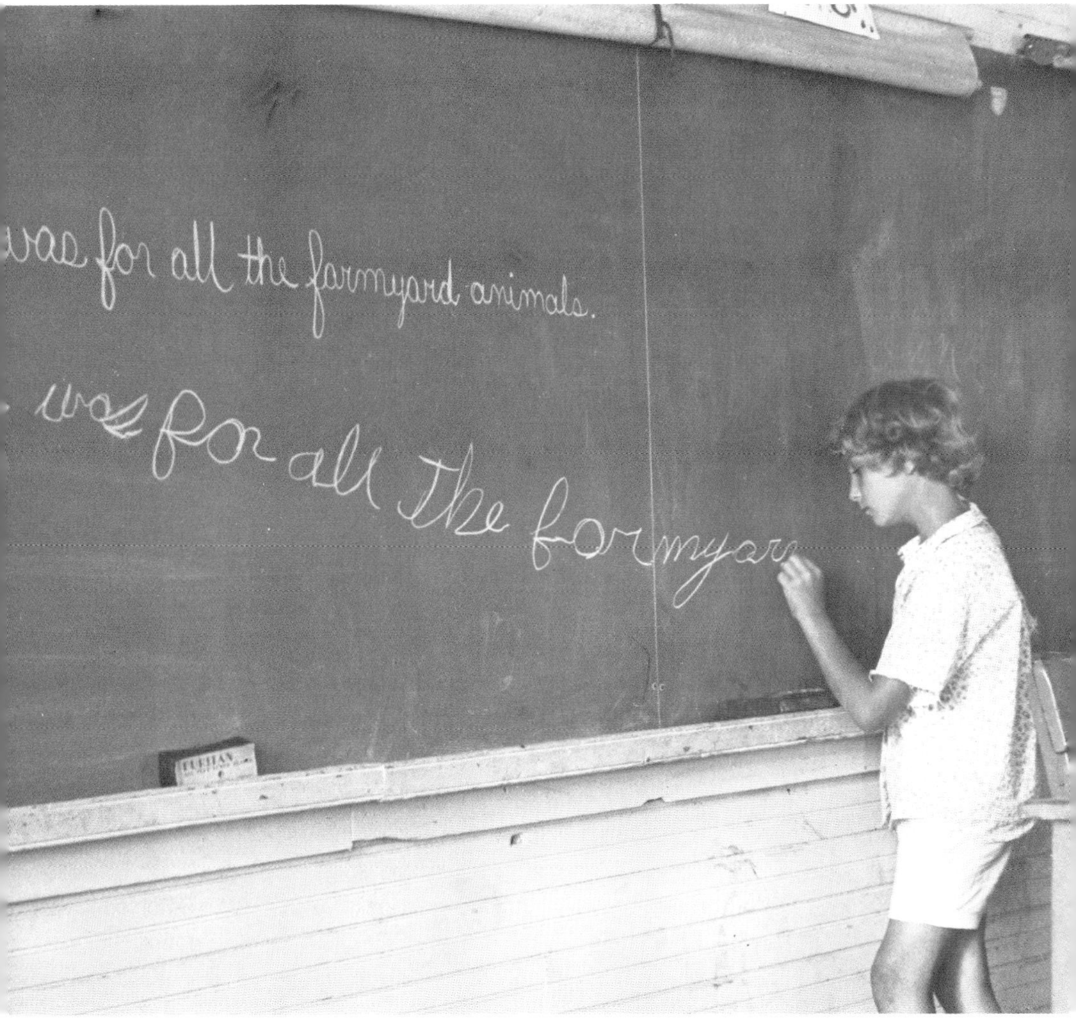

Spring

"If you live according to my laws, if you keep my commandments and put them into practice, I will give you the rain you need at the right time; the earth shall give its produce and the trees of the countryside their fruits . . . "

Leviticus 26:3-4

There aren't many covered bridges left in the mountains, and yet they have served the region well. The horses are not afraid to cross through them. The roof protects the wood from weathering, and the traveler won't get drenched in a thundershower. The old spans blend nicely into the landscape. A covered bridge is so much more human than a concrete one. And it is truly Appalachian; it symbolizes how folks are supposed to help their neighbors who have to cross the dangerous streams of life.

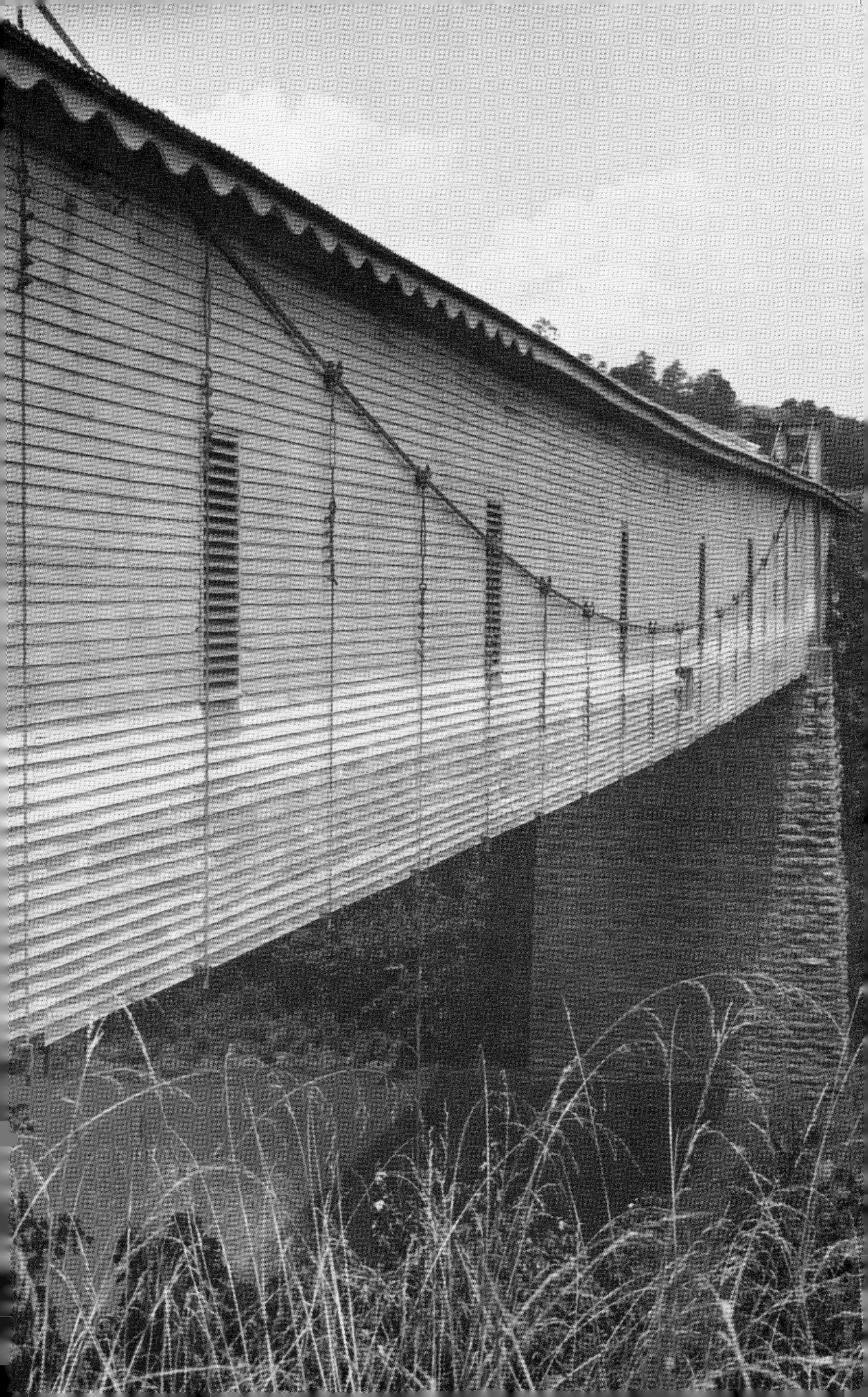

Spring

I lift my eyes to the mountains:
where is help to come from?
Help comes to me from Yahweh,
who made heaven and earth.

Psalm 121:1-2

    I climbed up and got a view from the mountain slope. It took my breath away and sent me soaring. I left the earth behind and shot out as if I were skipping on the hilltops. But the release was only for a moment, because I soon found myself once again on the sun-warmed granite.

    No, I don't have wings. I am earthbound in my powers and worries. And yet in another moment I found myself aloft again, but this time in God's great arms; for what I lack in physical ways I now make up in simple prayer. Let the land be witness to this.

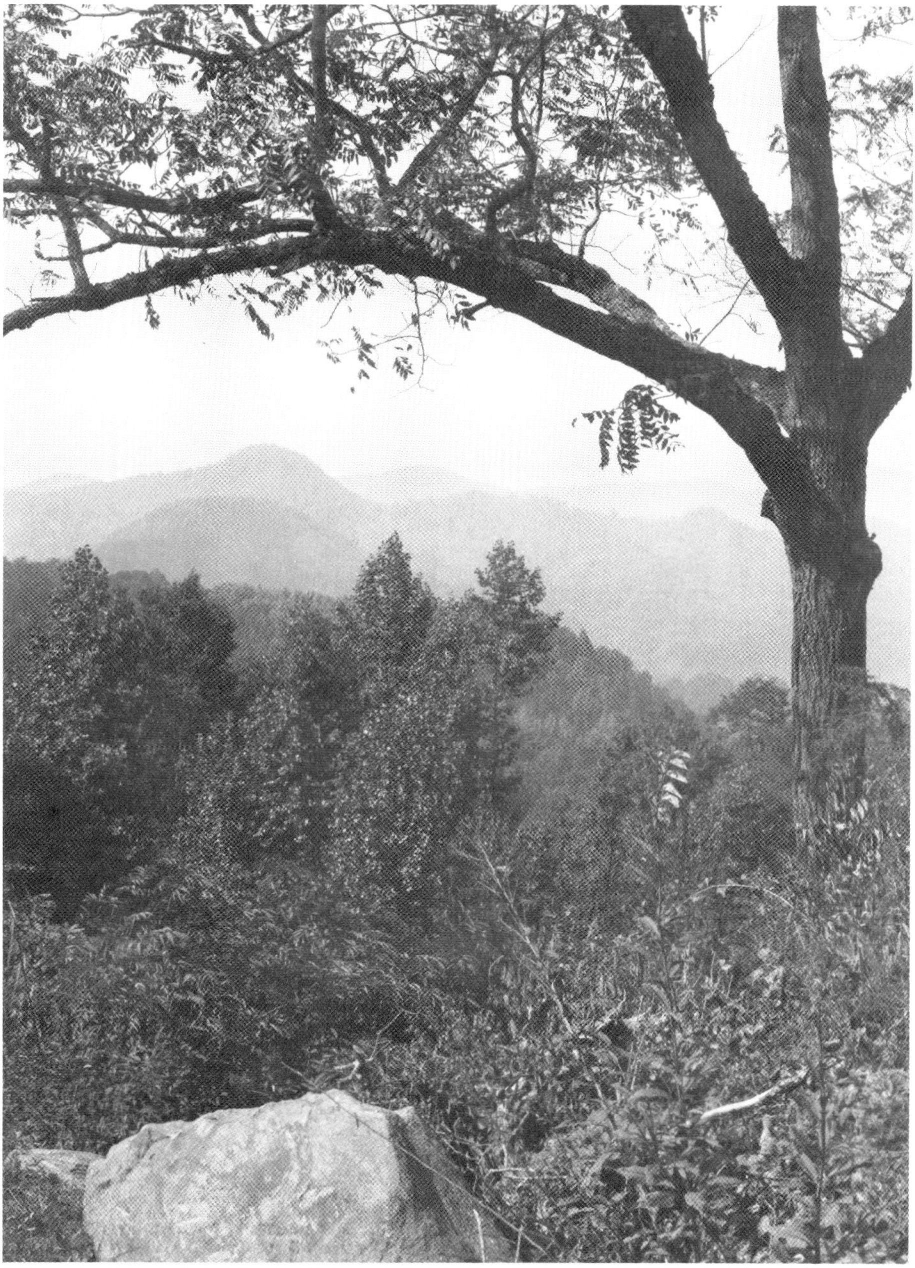

Spring

This love of yours is like a morning cloud, like the dew that quickly disappears.

Hosea 6:4

My, we hated to see them go. They were fine folks, but they just couldn't make it. Kids were all about—some on swings, some in the puddles, some racing around. Those people used all the buildings, the tools, the fields. But they needed money, and now they have gone up North. Were they really so unattached? Did they just fade away, or will they return when they find life isn't so good up there? Maybe soon. The land can still grow crops, and the place could be patched up. We just hope and pray and know that someday they will be back.

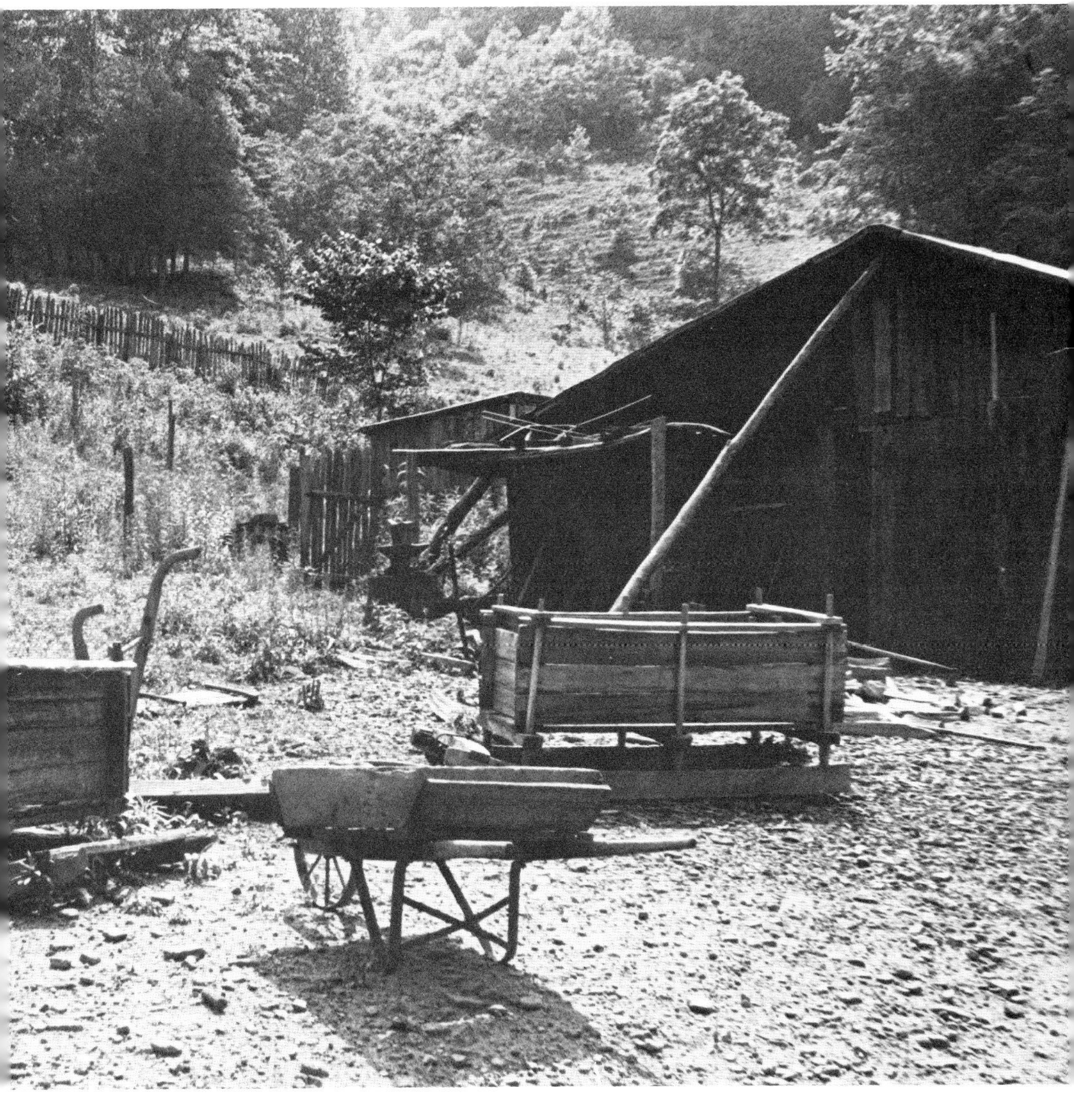

Spring

*How beautiful on the mountains,
are the feet of one who brings good
   news,
who heralds peace, brings happiness,
proclaims salvation, and tells Zion,
   "Your God is king!"*

Isaiah 52:7

  Is coal the king of the region? For some people coal is a paycheck and food on the table. For those who risk the rock falls and the black lung, there's a certain nobility in the black stuff. However, the relationship is both love and hate. At times there's boom, at times there's bust. And it takes a strong back to mine the seam, and a careful hand to keep the place safe. Coal might be king; but the good news is, there is a greater King.

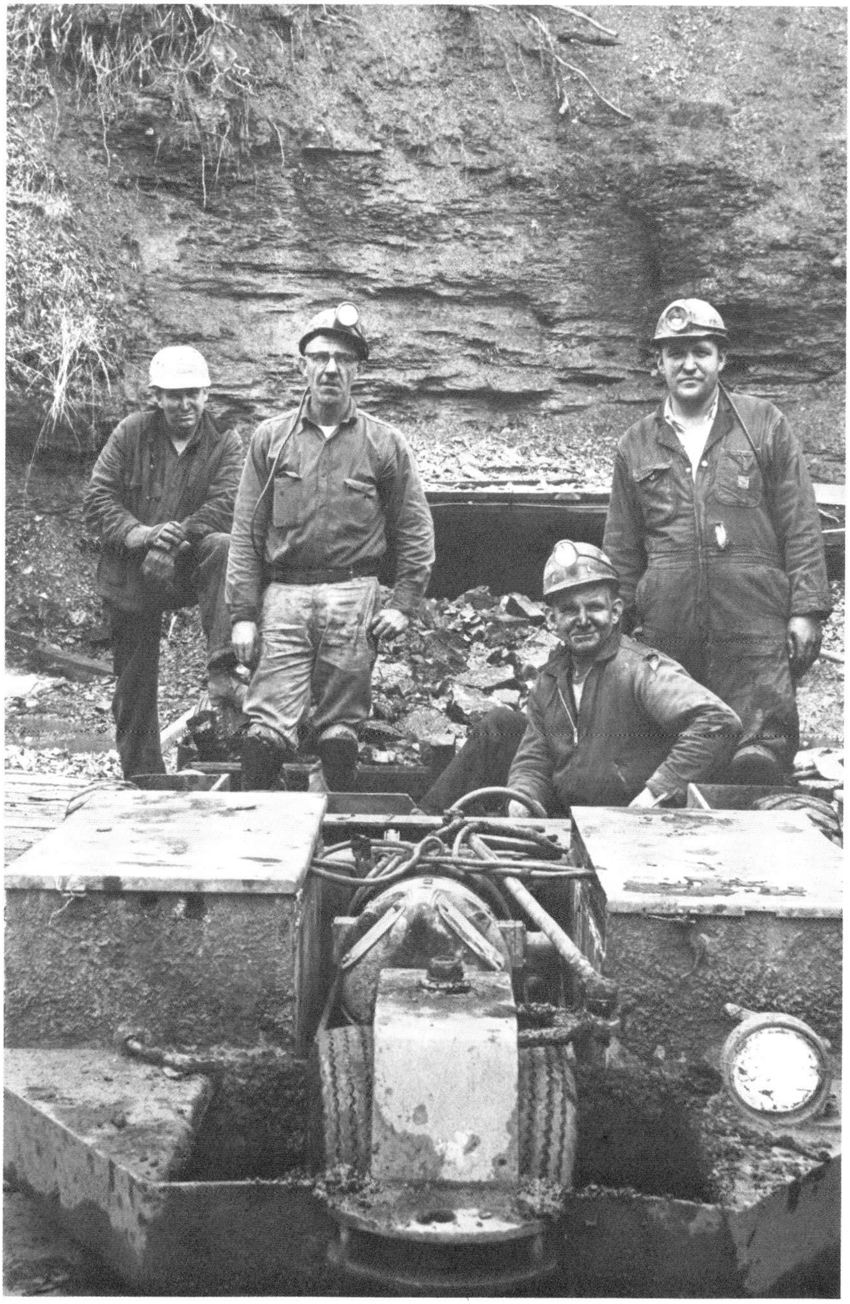

Spring

"Now I am making the whole of creation new."

Revelation 21:5

Worshipers praise the Creator for all good things. But the work of creation is not finished. We have become co-creators of the earth itself. We enter into a renewing act, and the earth itself is refashioned into something new. We don't just come to watch, to listen, and be passive; we enter into the worship as a people with a task. We need vitality so we can be active in the proper sense. We share a few sacred moments in order to gain the strength to move our mountain of troubles.

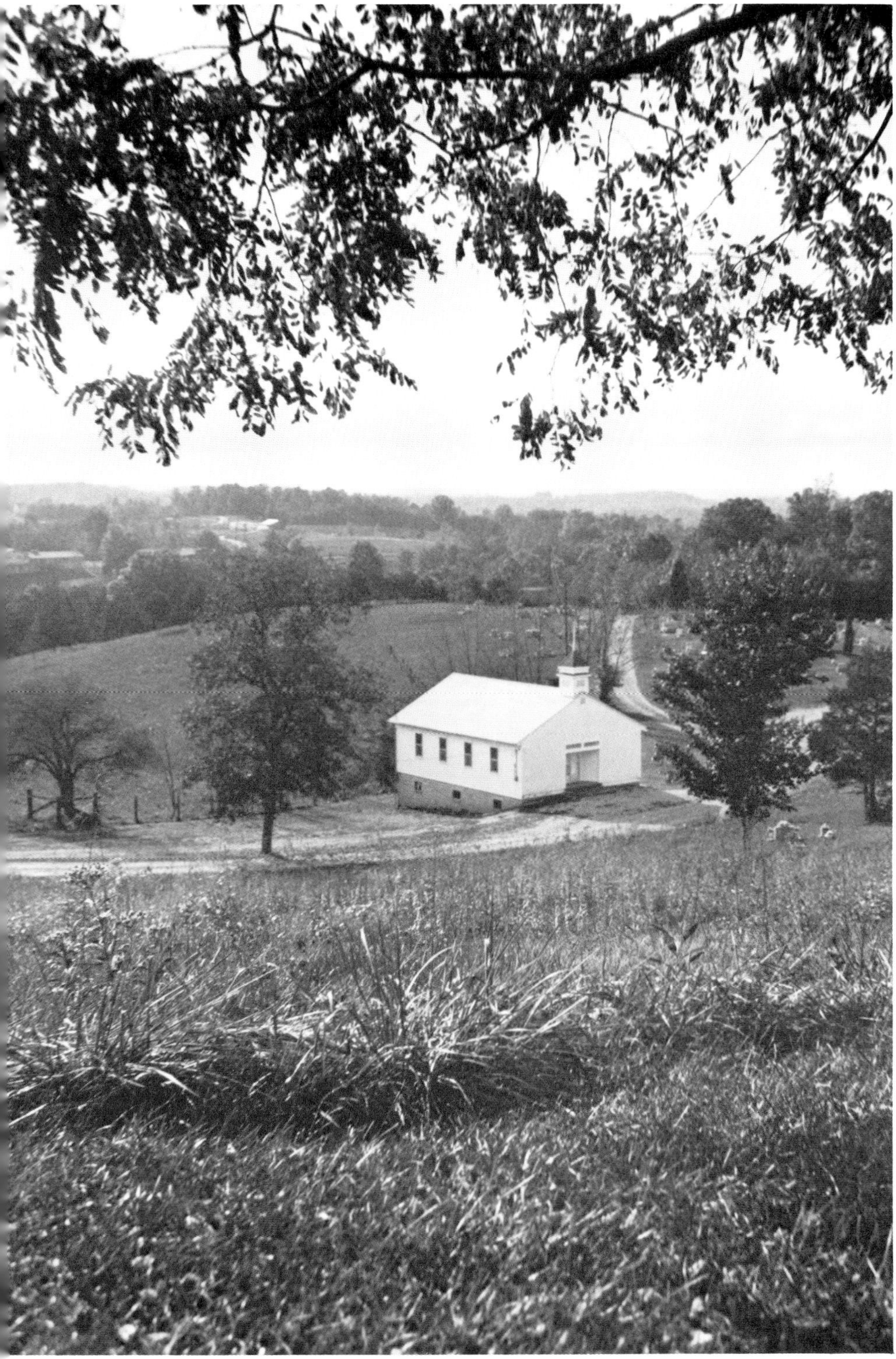

Spring

Of its own accord the land produces first the shoot, then the ear, then the full grain in the ear.

Mark 4:28

The land shares its life with us. From the soil plants furnish us with fruit, berries, nuts, and food of every kind. Appalachian soil has the ability to do this for years to come, if only we will take proper care of it. One important stage in the development of soil is the fragile wetlands. They seem so useless at first glance, but actually they teem with life. They deserve our respect and protection.

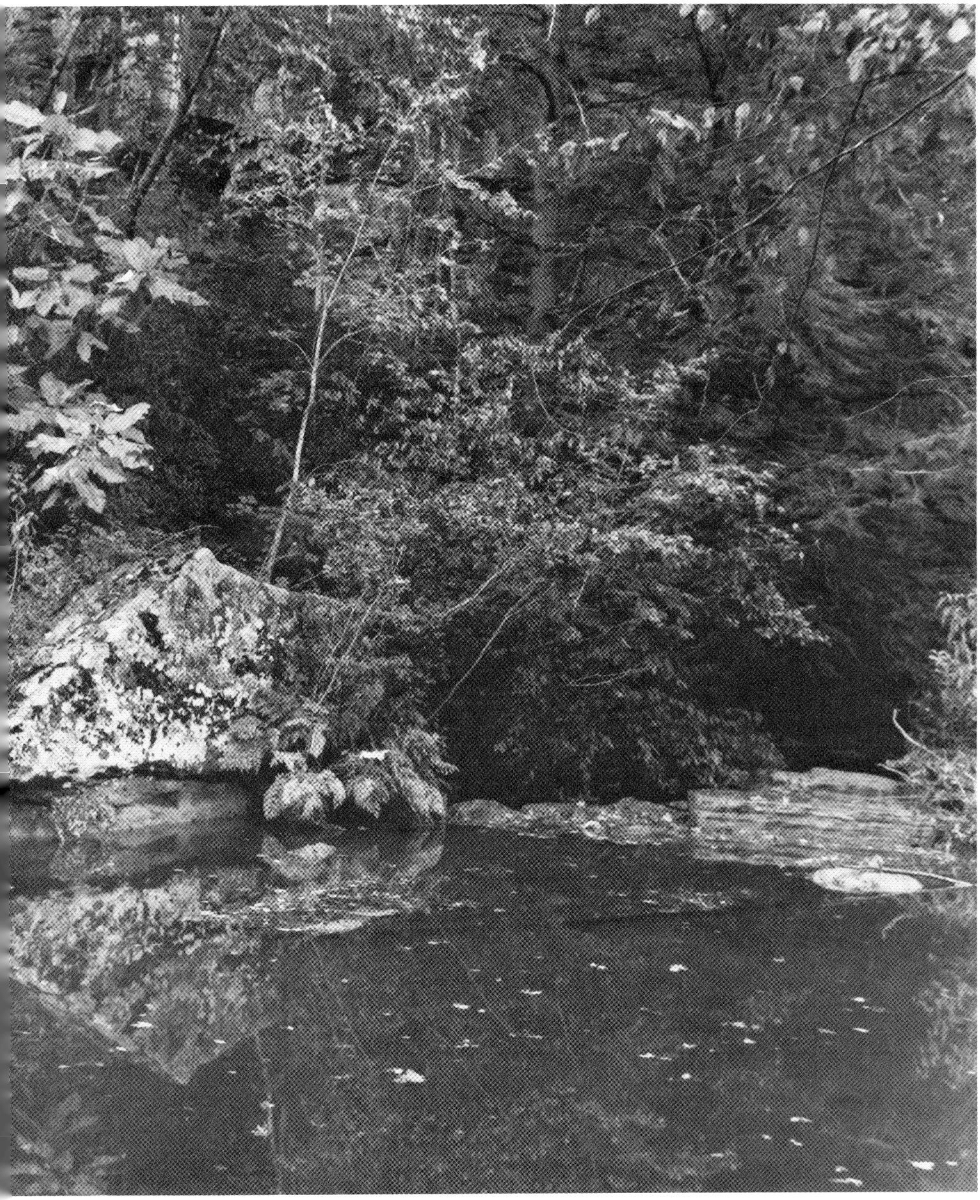

Spring

Send victory like a dew, you heavens,
　and let the clouds rain it down.
Let the earth open for salvation to
　spring up.
Let deliverance, too, bud forth
　which I, Yahweh, shall create.
　　　　　　　　　　Isaiah 45:8

What does a flower mean to me? Sometimes I hardly notice flowers; there are so many. Yet they are more than simple gifts. They are the ornaments of the earth. They make me lighthearted. They are a sign that the earth and I are one. They color the drabness that my human carelessness has wrought. They tell me that what is momentary has a value. And they give me hope of final victory.

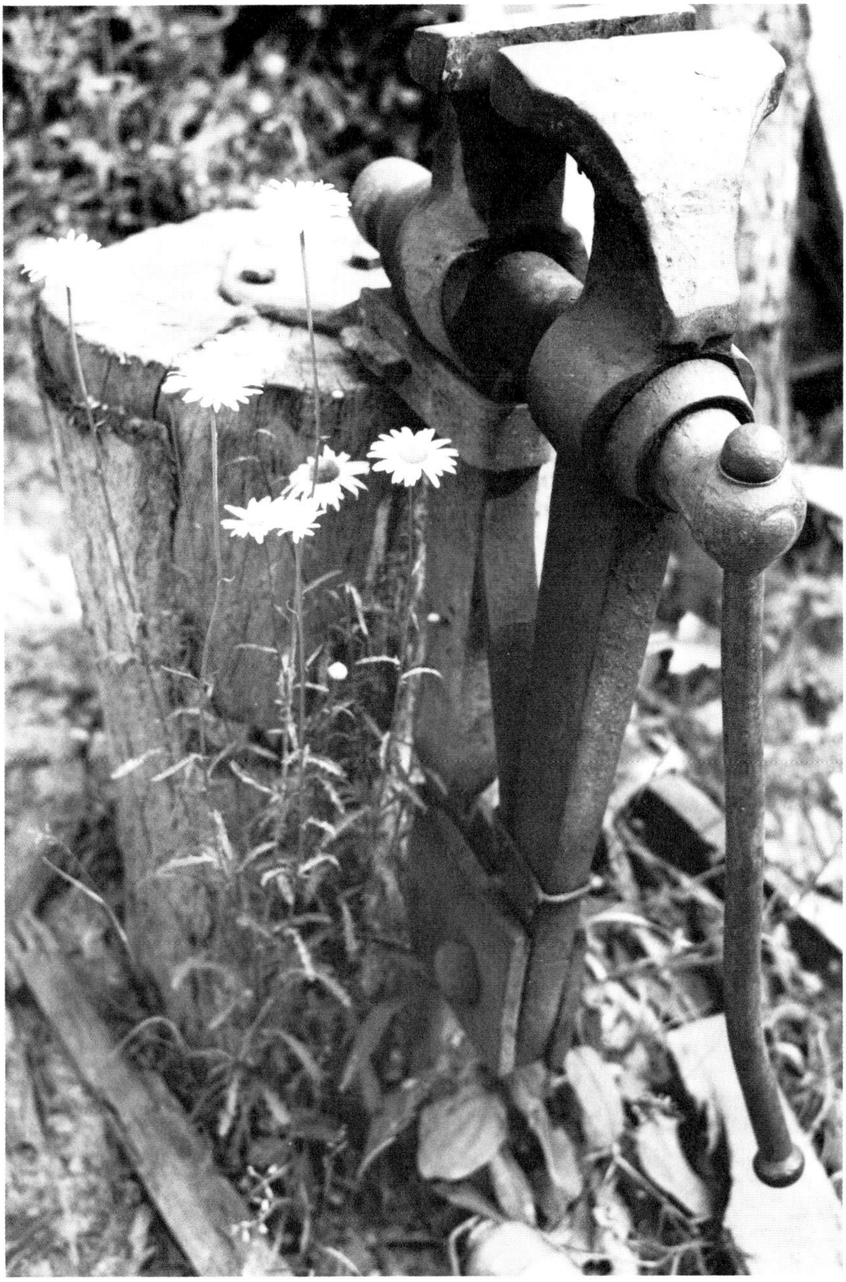

Spring

*She deploys her strength from one end
 of the earth to the other,
ordering all things for good.*
Wisdom 8:1

      We can find strength in many parts of creation. March winds, April tornadoes, landslides after a heavy rain, rushing rivers, the hawk grabbing its prey, tree roots breaking a rock. And we find strong people as well: those with will power to sustain hardships; those with resolute minds and hearts; the brave who endure their own illness and that of their kin and friends. The one who faces death cheerfully has inner strength when physical powers fail. All of these teach us to discover our own strengths and forge them well.

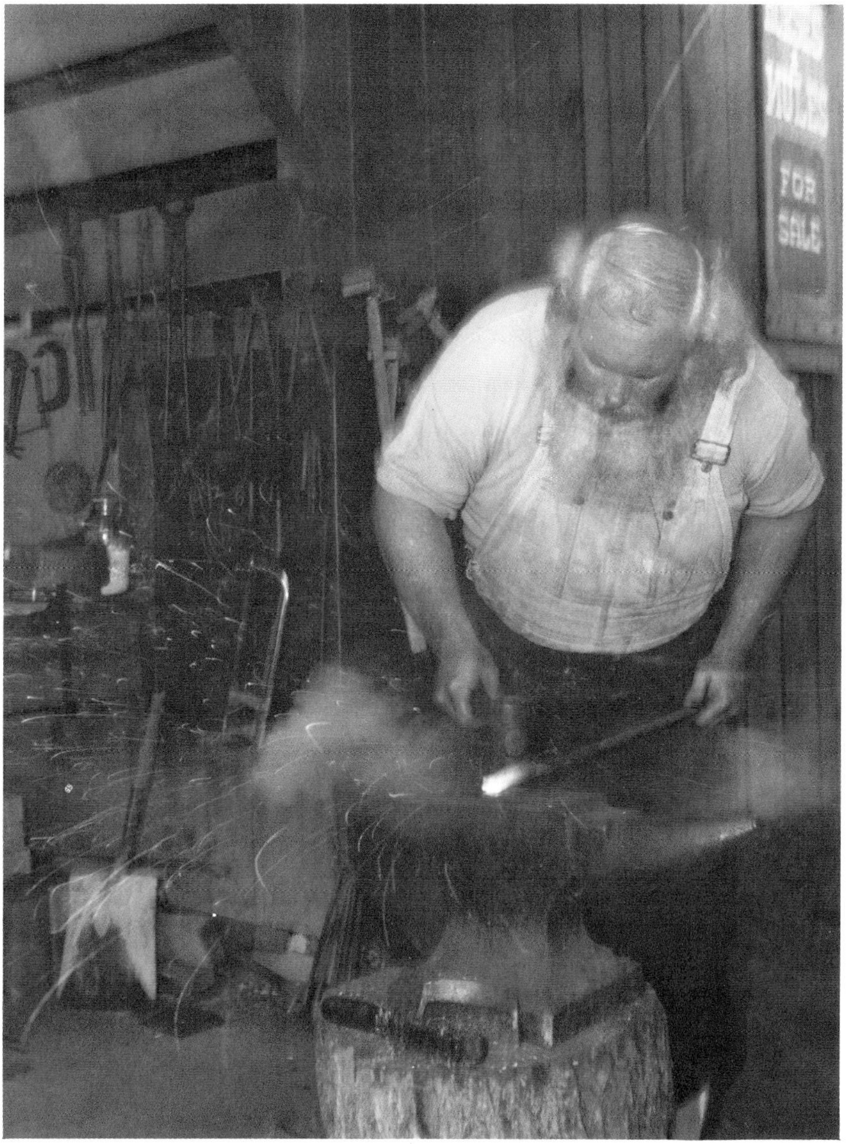
FOR
SALE

Spring

*On the seventh day God completed the
    work he had been doing.
He rested on the seventh day after all the
    work he had been doing.*

Genesis 2:2

"Those biscuits and gravy faded a long time back. It's the roots that have done me in. They cling like cats on a wool sweater. They tie the earth up in knots and give it funny ideas. It seems to say, 'I just want to be left alone.' Why can't it see that when the roots are gone it's free? When plowed and harrowed it'll breathe again and grow a better stand of corn."

"Yes, I'm tuckered out from bustin' sod, and I'm not alone. The good Lord got a little bushed in makin' these hills. That's why he took the Sabbath off."

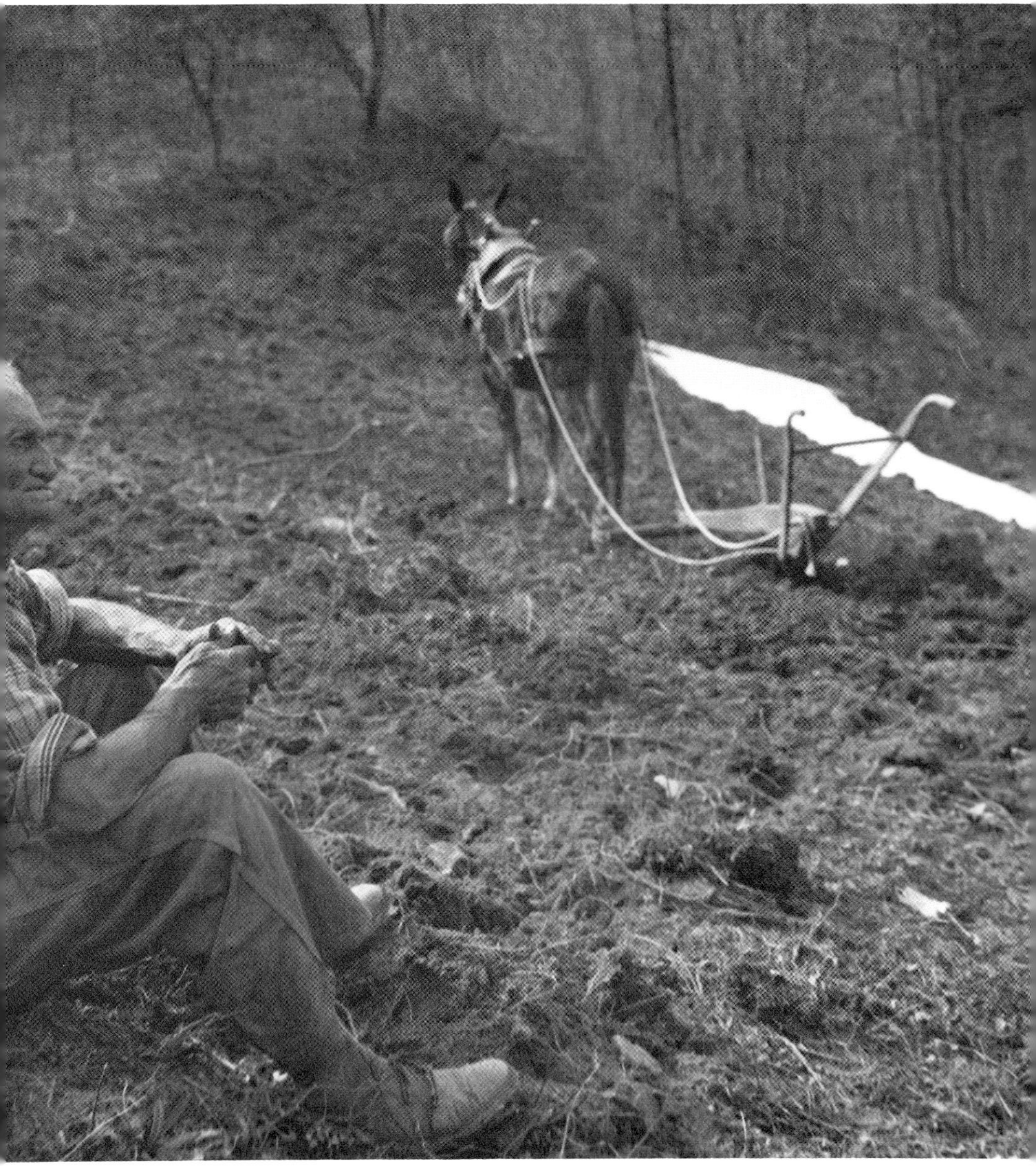

Spring

He will love you and bless you and
  increase your numbers;
He will bless the fruit of your body and
  the produce of your soil . . .
                              Deuteronomy 7:13

      Ducks are Appalachian favorites. They float and swim and bob about; they flap and honk and fly in "V" formation; they waddle about the shore with a mountain flare. They come, stay awhile, eat our grain, and slip away—like our city kin. Maybe ducks can teach us lightheartedness. In fact, all birds and wildlife will be our teachers if we can be humble enough to learn from them. They invite us to watch them and admire them—in ways other than through a gunsight.

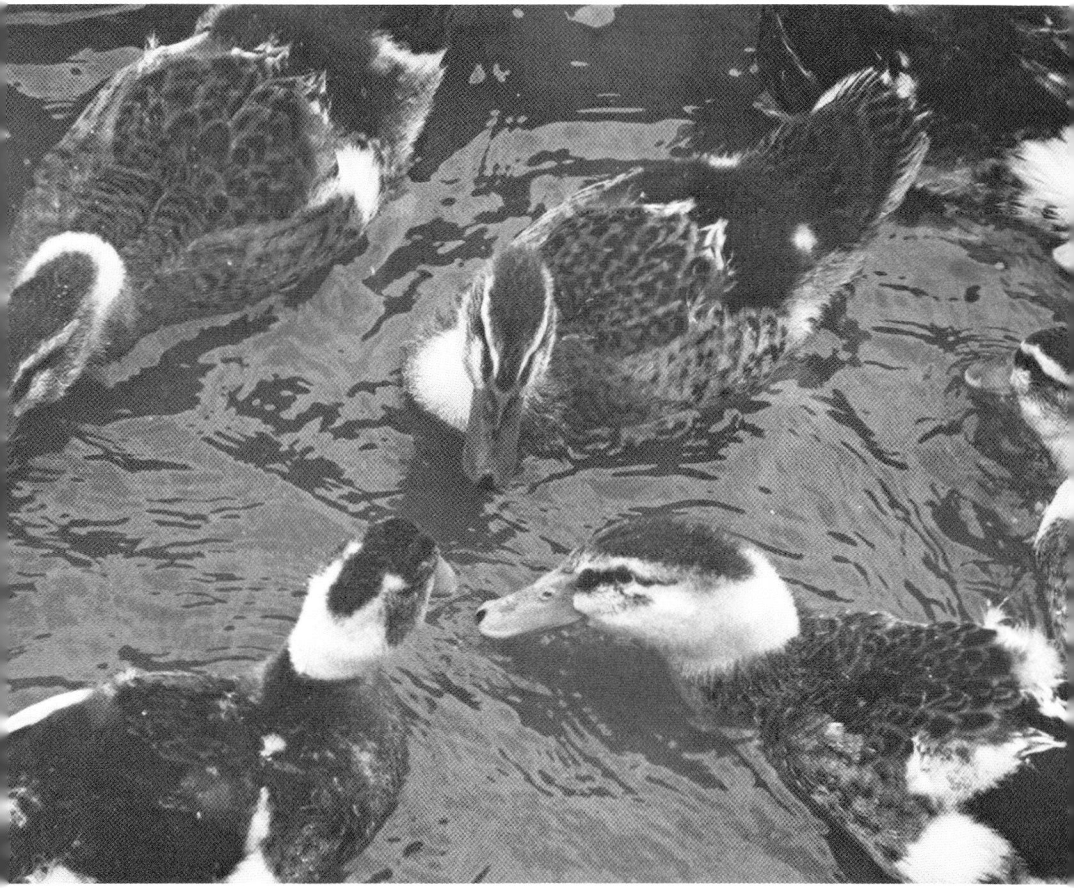

Spring

There is always hope for a tree:
　when felled, it can start its life again;
　its shoots continue to sprout.
Its roots may be decayed in the earth,
　its stump withering in the soil,
but let it scent the water, and it buds,
　and puts out branches like a plant new set.

Job 14:7-9

  We needn't go to distant places to find the Holy Land. It is right here, for all land is sacred on the face of the earth. In some mysterious way all land helped to soak up His blood and sweat; and nourished thus, it has burst into recreated glory. It was purchased at so high a price. And the work is not over yet; the battle goes on. And we are not merely spectators of a distant event; we are caught up in making this land holy—and keeping it so for the yet unborn. That is our task and our hope on this ever-fresh Easter morn.

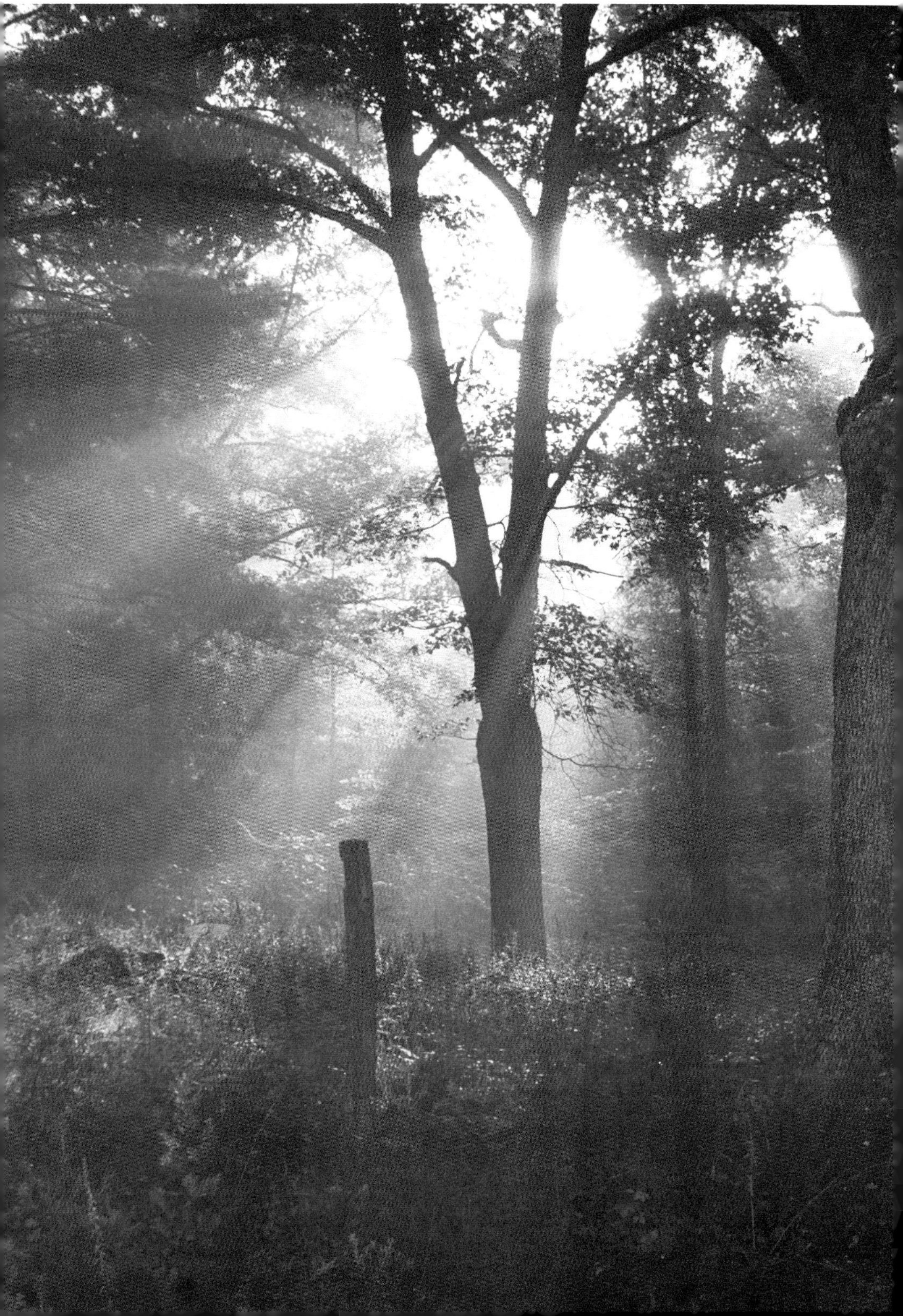

Spring

*Let the heavens be glad, let the earth
　rejoice,
let the sea thunder and all that it holds,
let the fields exult and all that is in them,
let all the woodland trees cry out for joy.*
　　　　　　　　　Psalm 96:11-12

　　　The hillsides are coming alive. Look closely. The sweat bees buzz, the crickets sound, flowers open wide. The sleeping land awakens with a burst of energy. A resurrection! The earth is reborn and stirs our inner spirits. We too can be renewed.

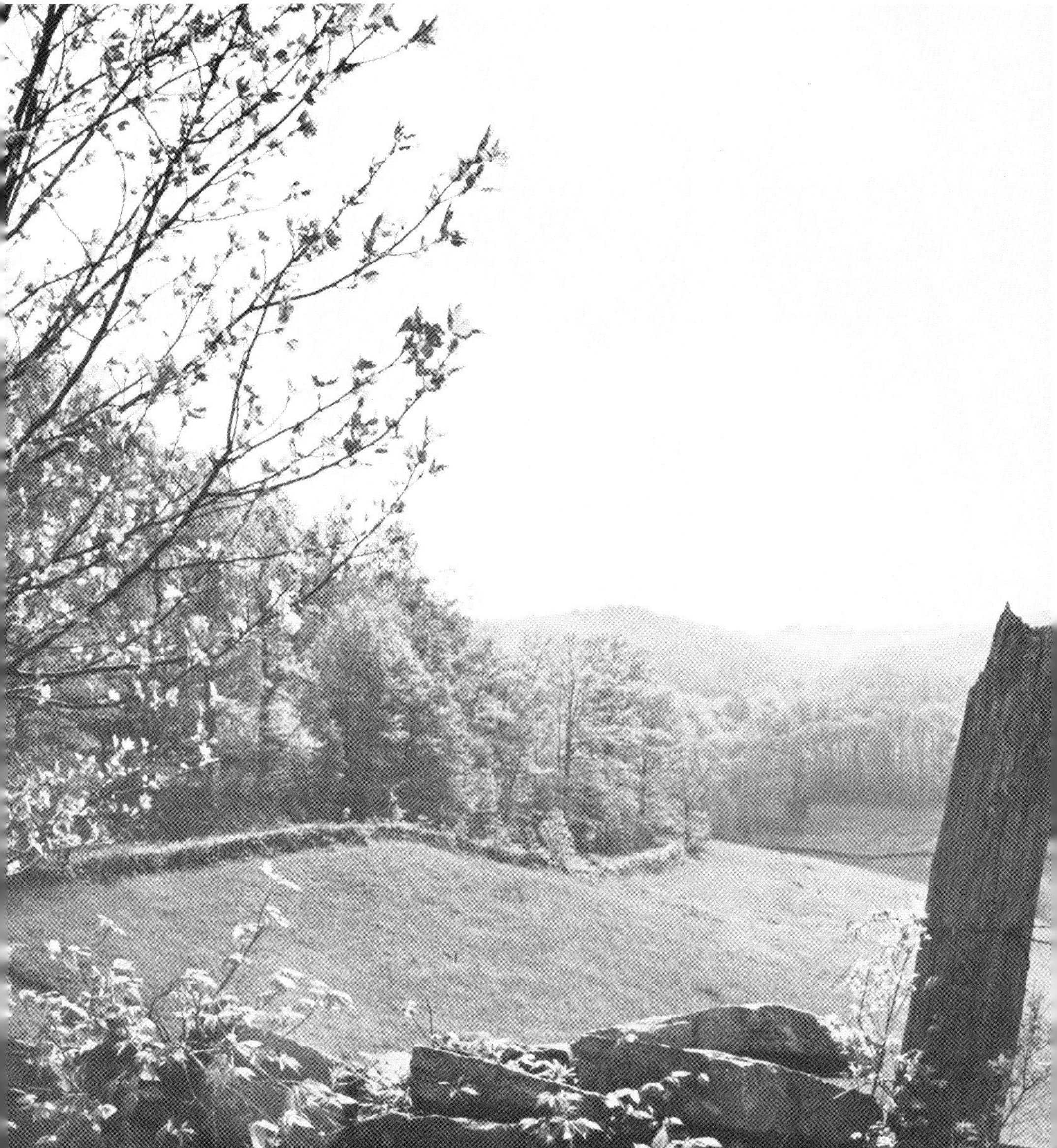

Spring

*Mountains and hills, orchards and forests,
wild animals and farm animals, snakes
  and birds,
all kings on earth and nations,
princes, all rulers in the world,
young men and girls,
old people, and children too!
Let them all praise the name of
Yahweh . . .*

                    Psalm 148:9-13a

    All creatures enjoy each other.
When we smile, does the earth smile too?
No, it's not that way, my friend. We smile
because the earth is smiling, and it smiles
because God is smiling all the time.

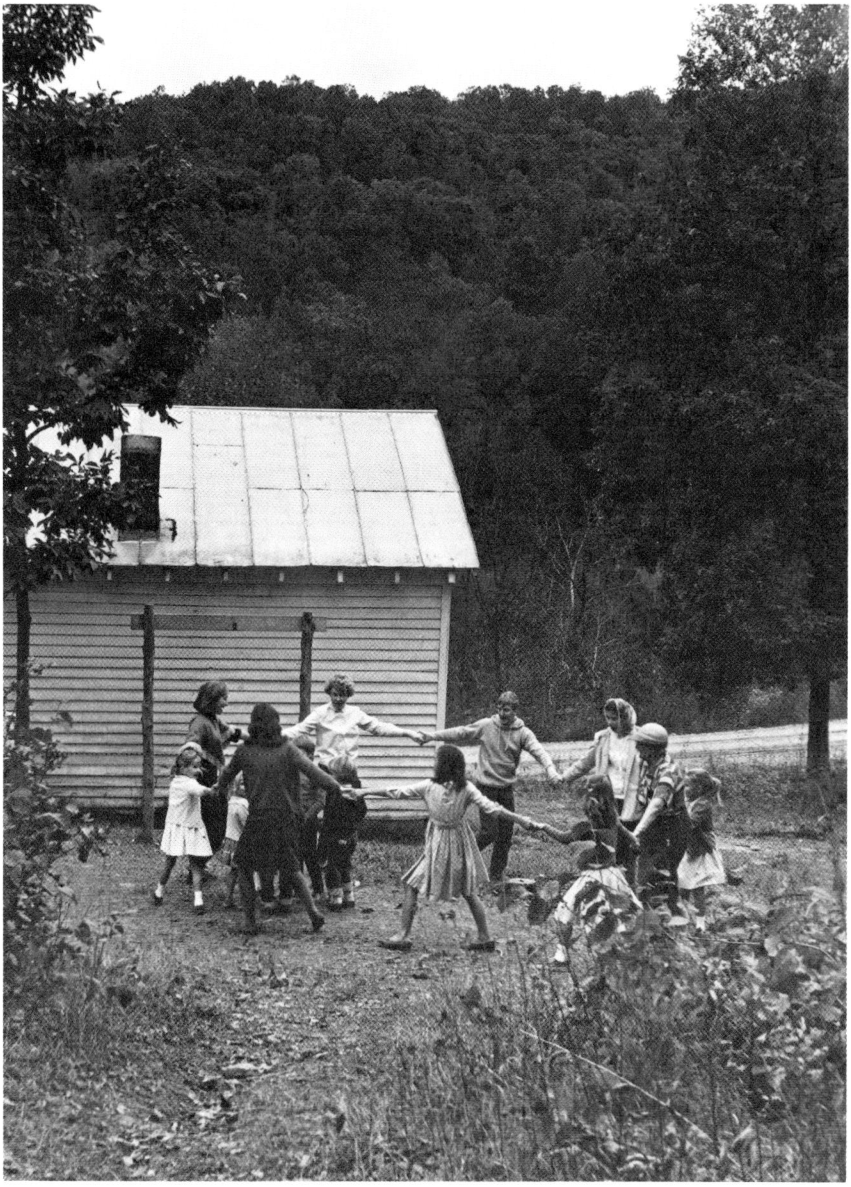

Spring

*Yes, you will leave with joy
  and be led away in safety.
Mountains and hills will break into joyful
  cries before you
and all the trees of the countryside clap
  their hands.*

Isaiah 55:12

    To listen well is the mark of a true friend—and listening is a habit we learn through years of freeing ourselves enough from ourselves to enter into another's world. What we seldom realize is that the earth itself is listening to us— and it speaks to us also, if we will only make the effort to listen. But the earth is old and it speaks quite softly.

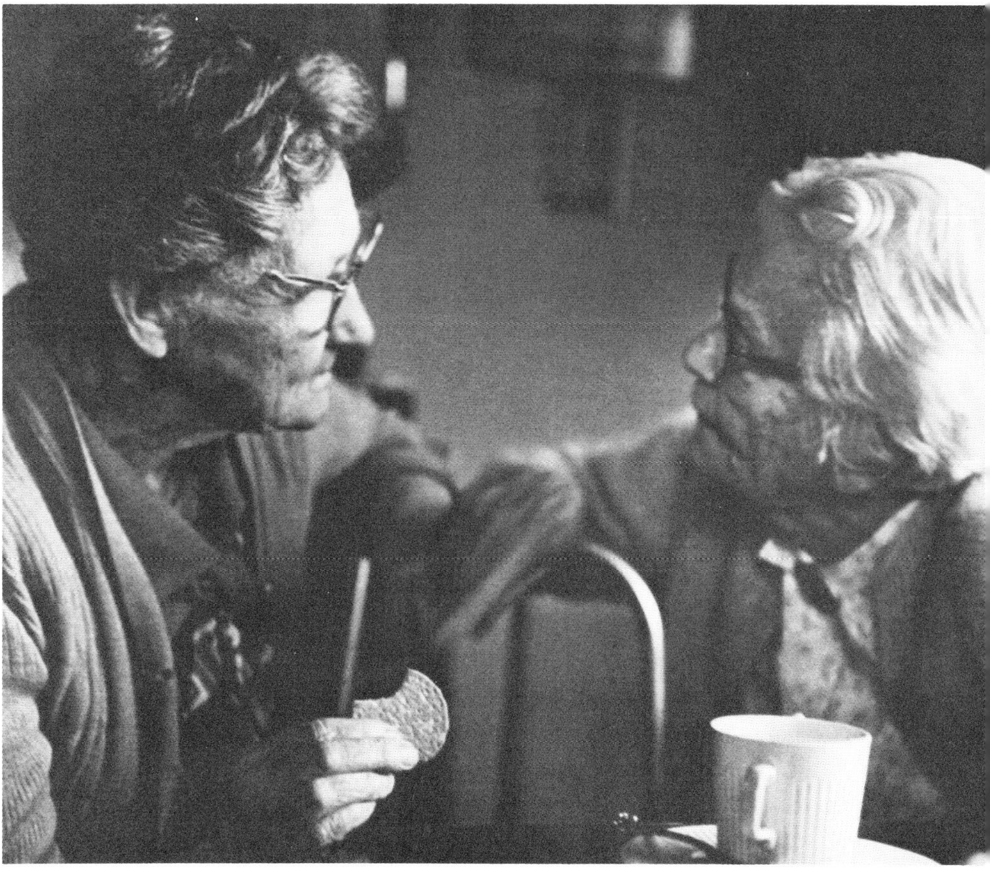

Spring

*Think of the flowers; they never have to
   spin or weave;
yet I assure you, not even Solomon in all
   his regalia
was robed like one of these.*

                        Luke 12:27

    We build our barriers which crumble, decay, and pass away. We worry and fret, toil and sweat. Yet we look around us and find majesty in earthly creatures which have no troubles. They tell us much. They clear our minds, quiet us down, and give us the time we need to hear the Lord who speaks.

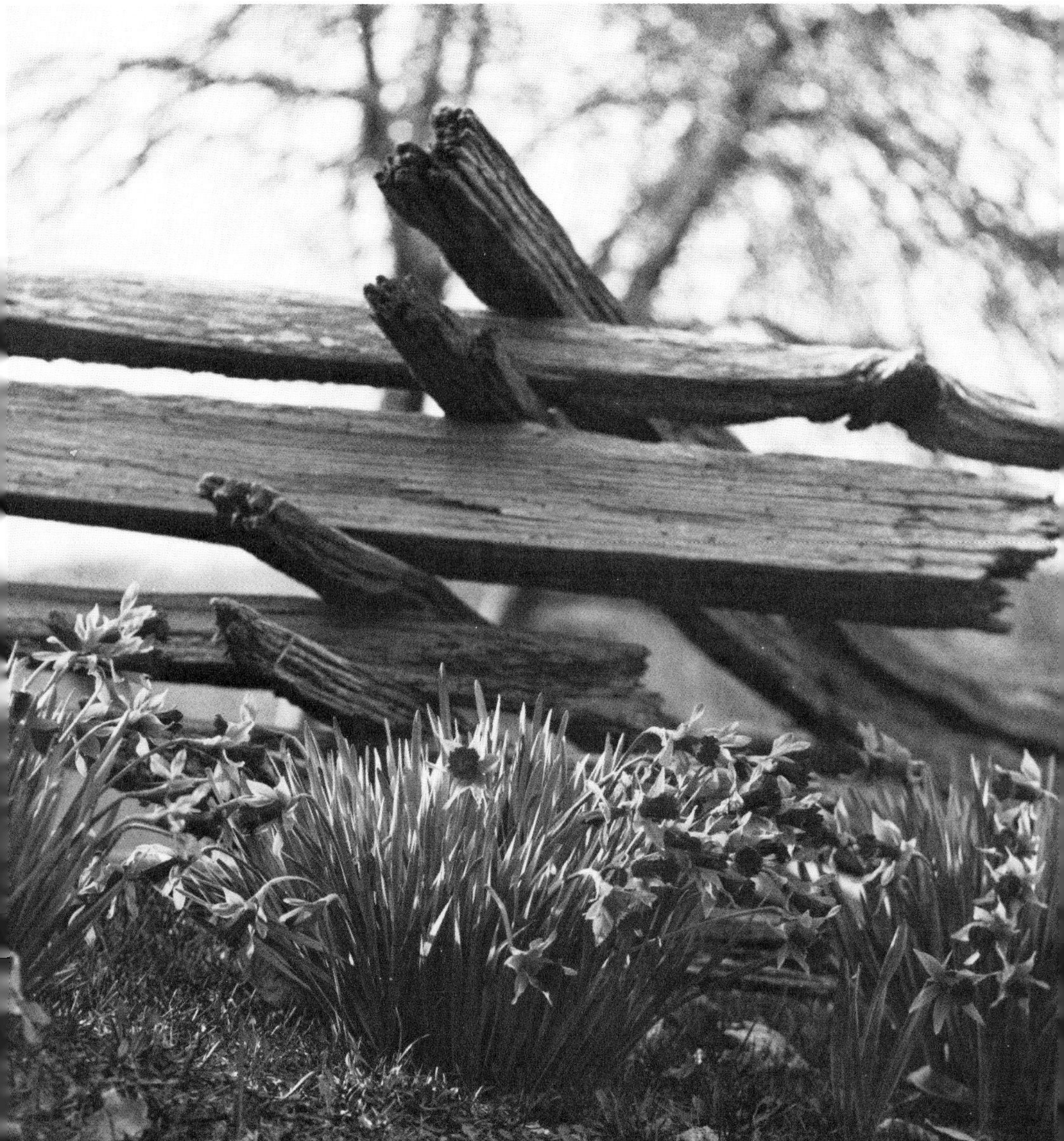

Spring

*He will do that by the same power with which
he can subdue the whole universe.*
                    Philippians 3:21b

When we're young we think we can do just about anything. Nothing's too big if we want to take it on. Where do we get such ideas? Maybe they're part of Appalachia. Our land is able to do many things in many ways. It is our recreational site, our place of rest and delight; it provides our daily food. If the land can do all this, why can't we? Is it wrong to want to be something—or to be more? We are so unsatisfied. But we will find rest eventually in God alone.

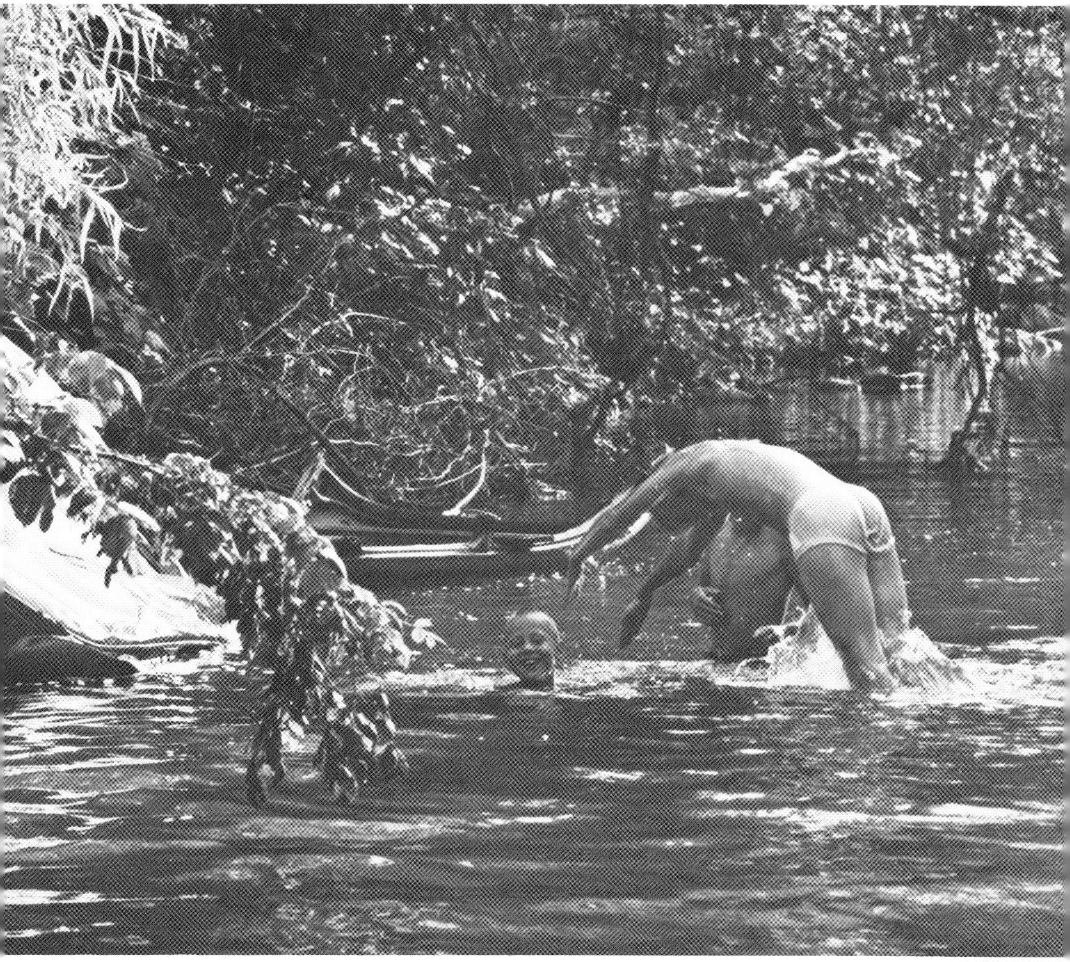

Spring

Shout for joy, you heavens;
exult, you earth!
You mountains, break into happy cries!
						Isaiah 49:13

      When fiddlers fiddle, they stamp their feet to the rhythm. Do you know why? It is because they are putting their music in tune with the earth. They connect with the rhythm of the earth through their feet, while they play the strings with their fingers. Crazy? Not so. Just get down on all fours next time you're at a hoedown and feel the vibrations.

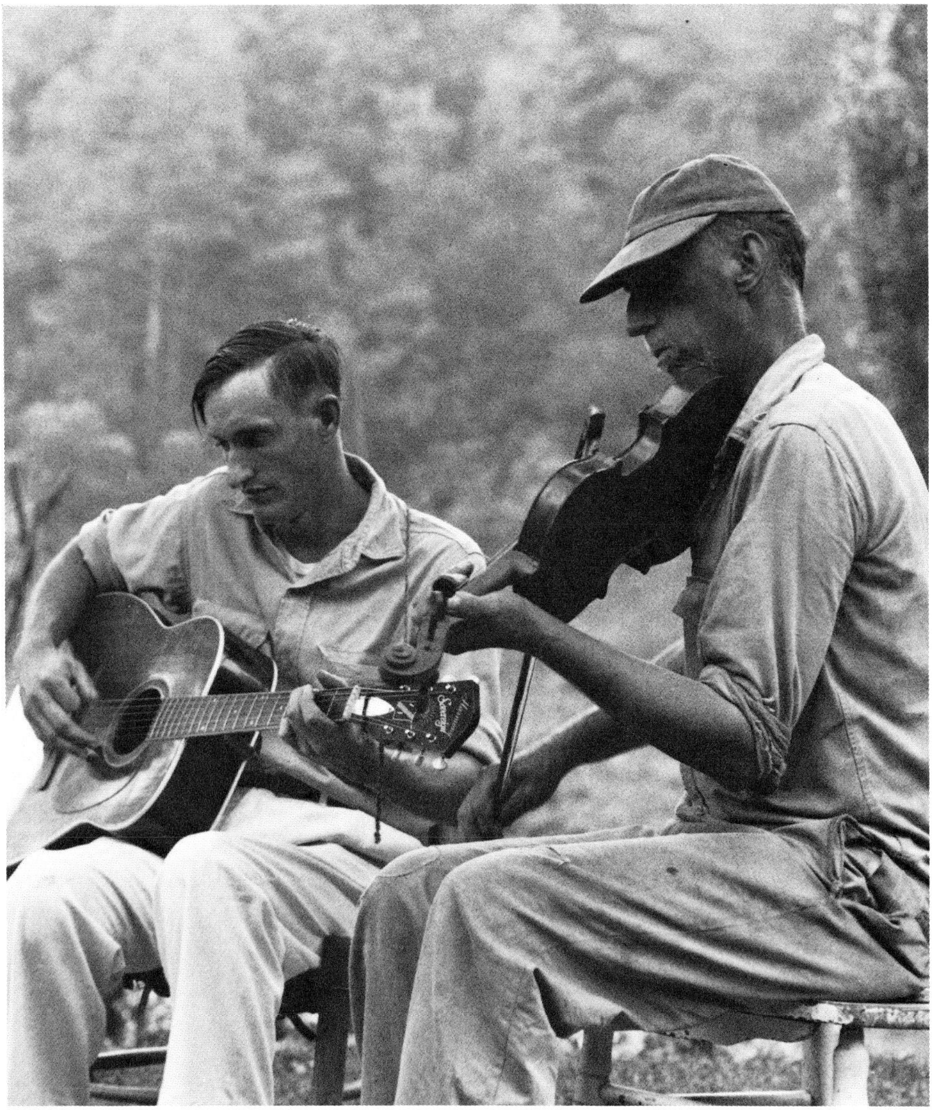

Summer

Summer

*God said, "See, I give you all the
  seed-bearing plants
that are upon the whole earth, and all
  the trees
with seed-bearing fruit; this shall be your
food."*

Genesis 1:29

      Summer is the time of growth. If we were to have an eternal winter, the seeds would not sprout and become corn. We would have no feed for the animals which produce our meat and eggs and milk; the pastures, orchards, and gardens would be barren. The Lord gives us summer sunshine, but through our wrongdoing we are able to create a nuclear winter.

  Let's act to ensure our summers.

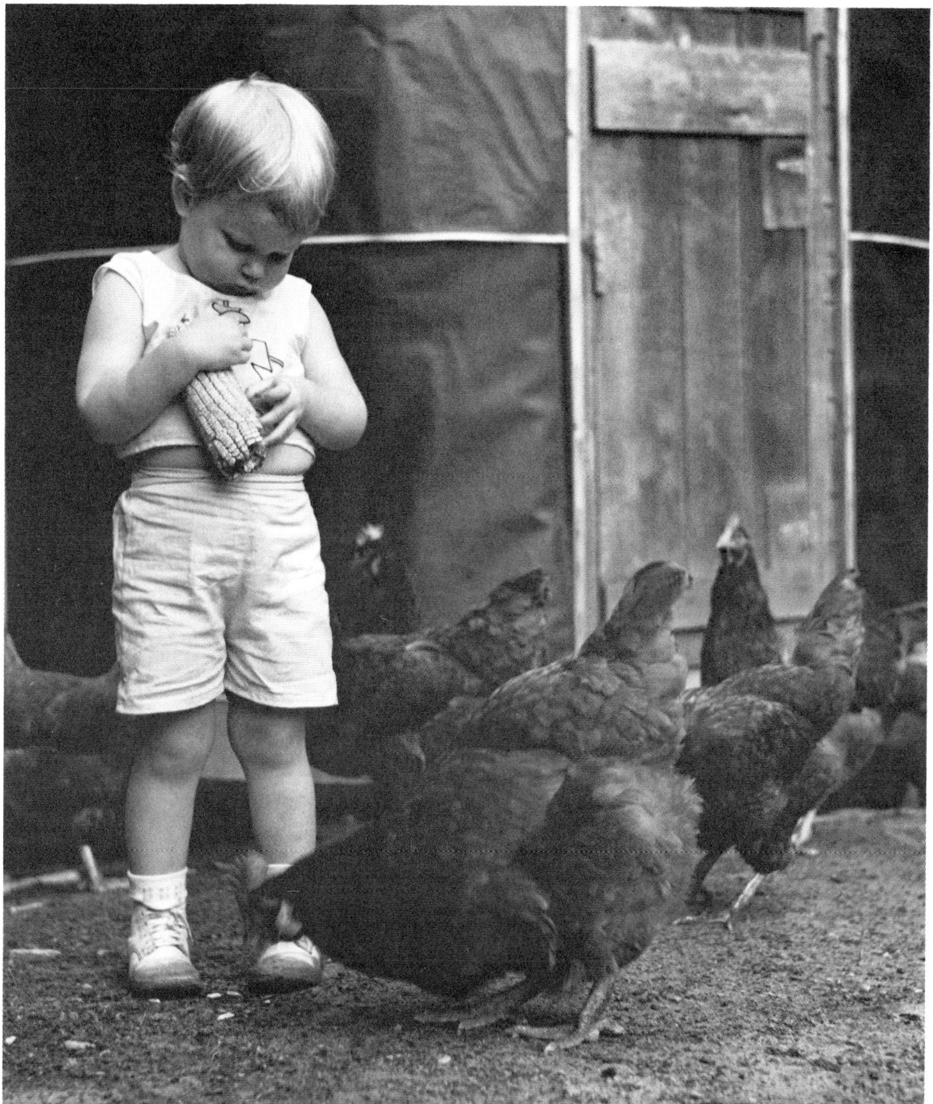

Summer

*Other (seeds) fell on rich soil and
    produced their crop,
some a hundredfold, some sixty, some
    thirty.*

> Matthew 13:8

  Children are our greatest treasure. They make the hills and mountains truly rich and fertile. Would the hills smile if there were no children? Mountain folks know the answer—and the answer doesn't come from book-learning. Everyone knows it takes a whole lot of faith, hope, and love to bring these kids to maturity.

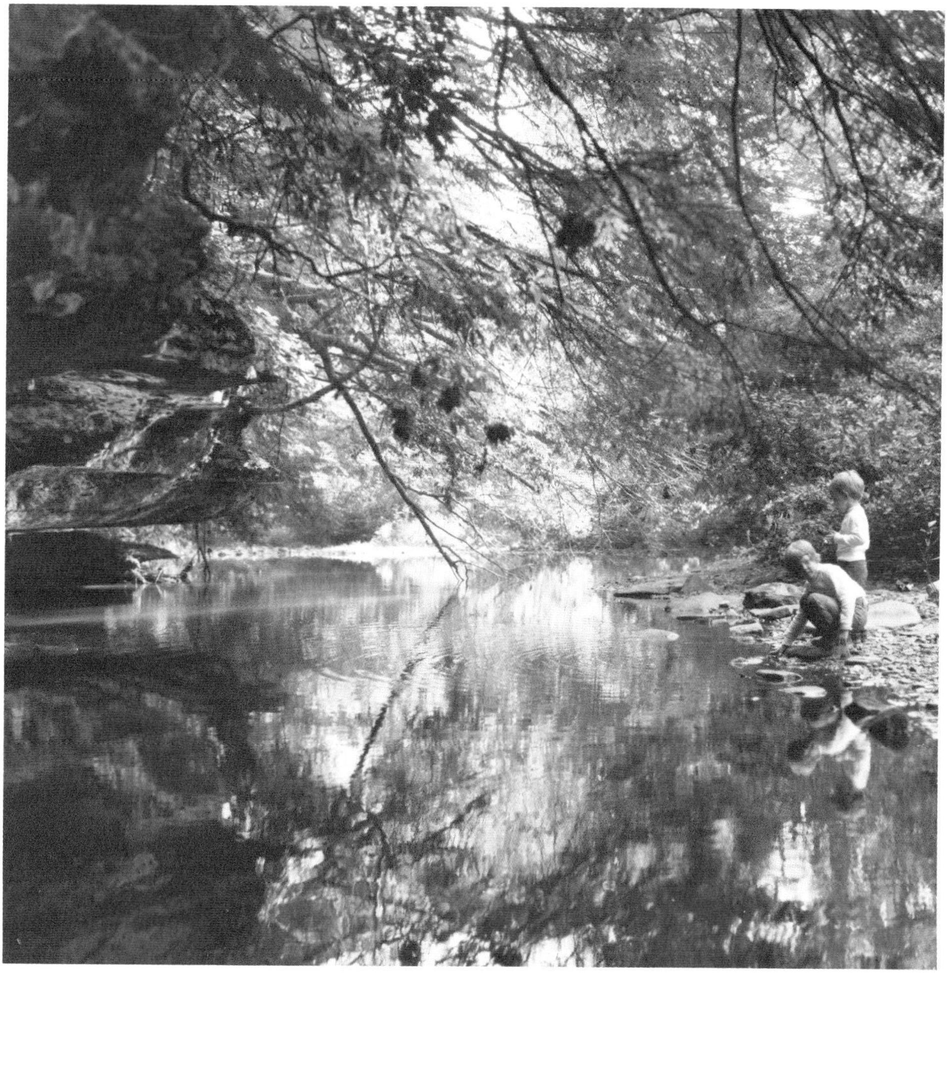

Summer

Then Yahweh said to Moses, "Now I will rain down bread for you from the heavens. Each day the people are to go out and gather the day's portion . . . "

Exodus 16:4

    The mill was once our manna-maker. The waters flowed over the rocks, through the race, and onto the wooden cups, which filled and turned the great wheel. The wheel, in turn, powered the millstone which ground the grains that our miller placed there. Stone-ground flour for our bread, the staff of life. The process was right here, simple and visible. Without the grain or the rain, without the wheel or the mill, we wouldn't have had bread. God provided—and so did we. All worked in harmony. Now the delivery truck brings trays full of plastic-wrapped enriched fluff. What became of our own bread? Our waterwheels?

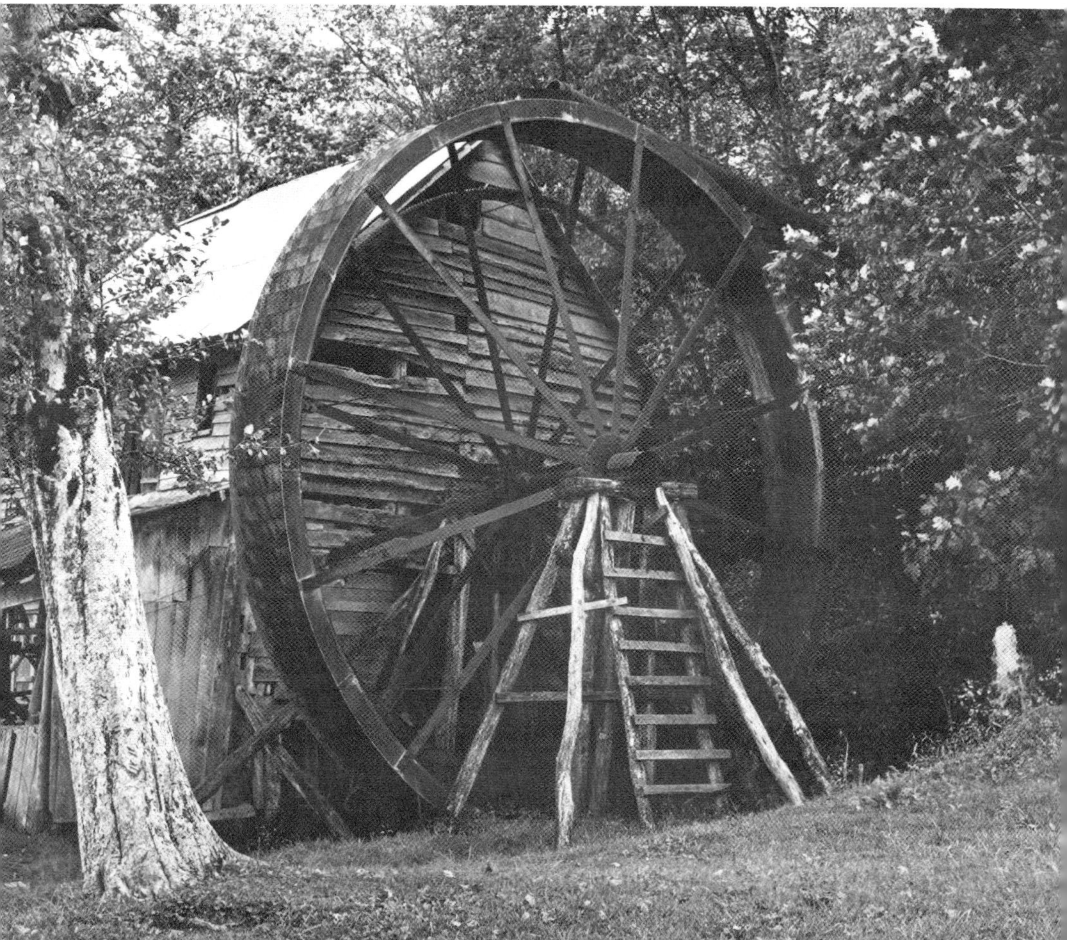

Summer

*I shall provide grass in the fields for
   your cattle,
and you will eat and have all you want.*
Deuteronomy 11:15

  Some people see the green slime and the rank weeds, and they fail to realize that the swamp is a treasure. Look a little closer. See the tadpoles, the dragonflies, the crickets. A whole world opens up before us at the micro level, which in some ways is as vast as the heavens above. Many forms of life flourish where earth and water mingle together.

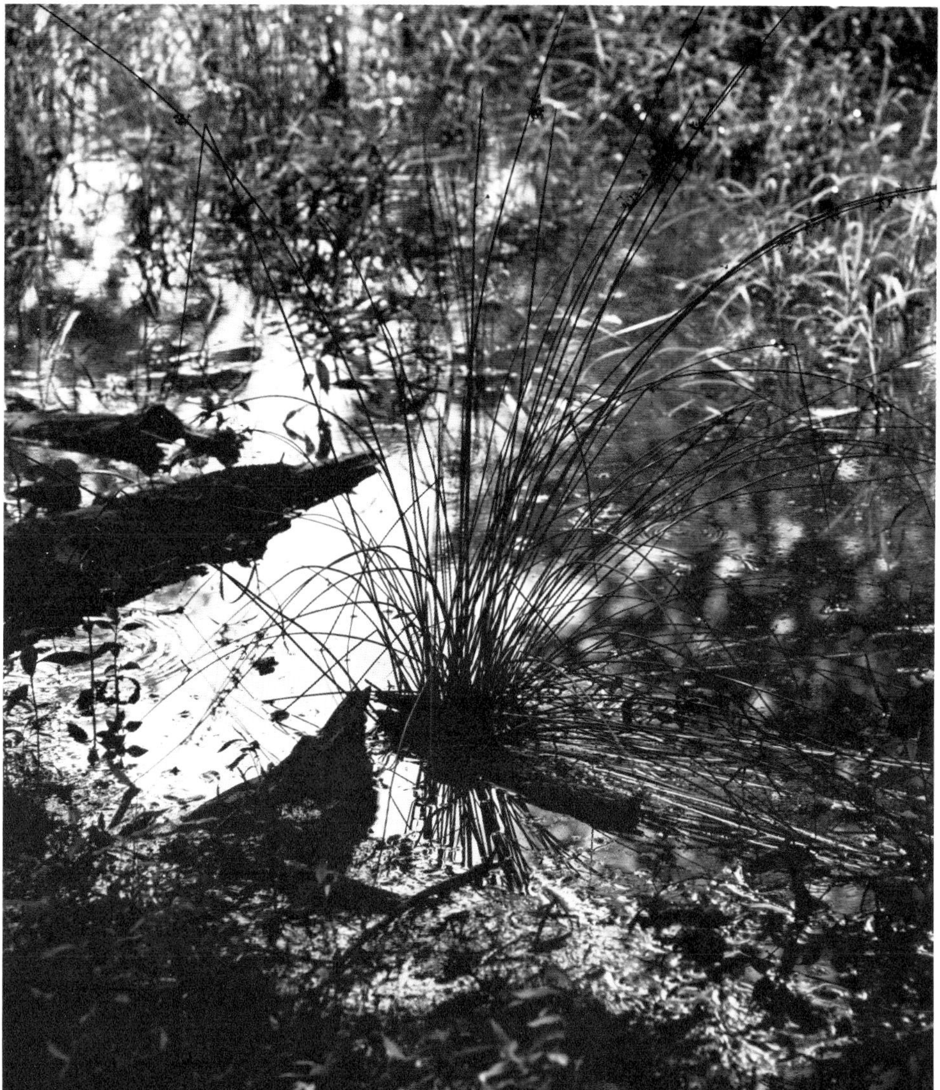

Summer

*Stand up and let the case begin
in the hearing of the mountains,
and let the hills hear what you say.*

Micah 6:1

     Our case is that we have changed the hills, conquered the mountains, crossed the streams, and cut down the woods. We stand as lords, but we are uncertain.

  Our deeds stand before the majestic hills. But the hills do not judge. If we treat the land well, we will gain our own respect. Knowing our limits, we will see ourselves not as conquerors but as stewards. We must be loving stewards of the woods, the creeks, the air, and the mountains. Only by serving the land and its inhabitants will we truly be "lords."

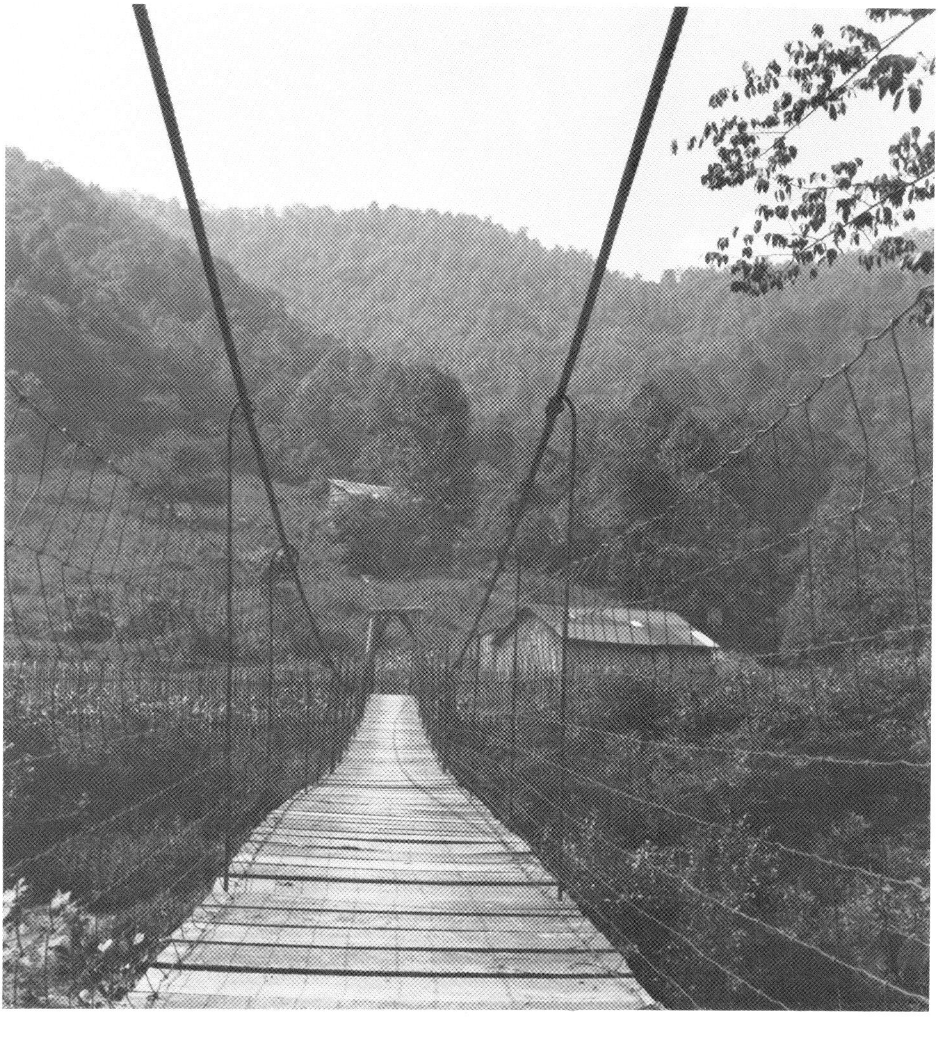

Summer

*No doubt of it, but God reveals wonders,
 and does great deeds that we cannot
 understand.
When he says to the snow, "Fall on the
 earth"
 or tells the rain to pour down in
 torrents,
he brings all men's strivings to a standstill
 so that each must acknowledge his
 hand at work.*

Job 37:5-7

  We each do our own thing. Outsiders call us independent people. We Appalachians have learned to make do; we earn our living; and sometimes we have the time just to sit and whittle.

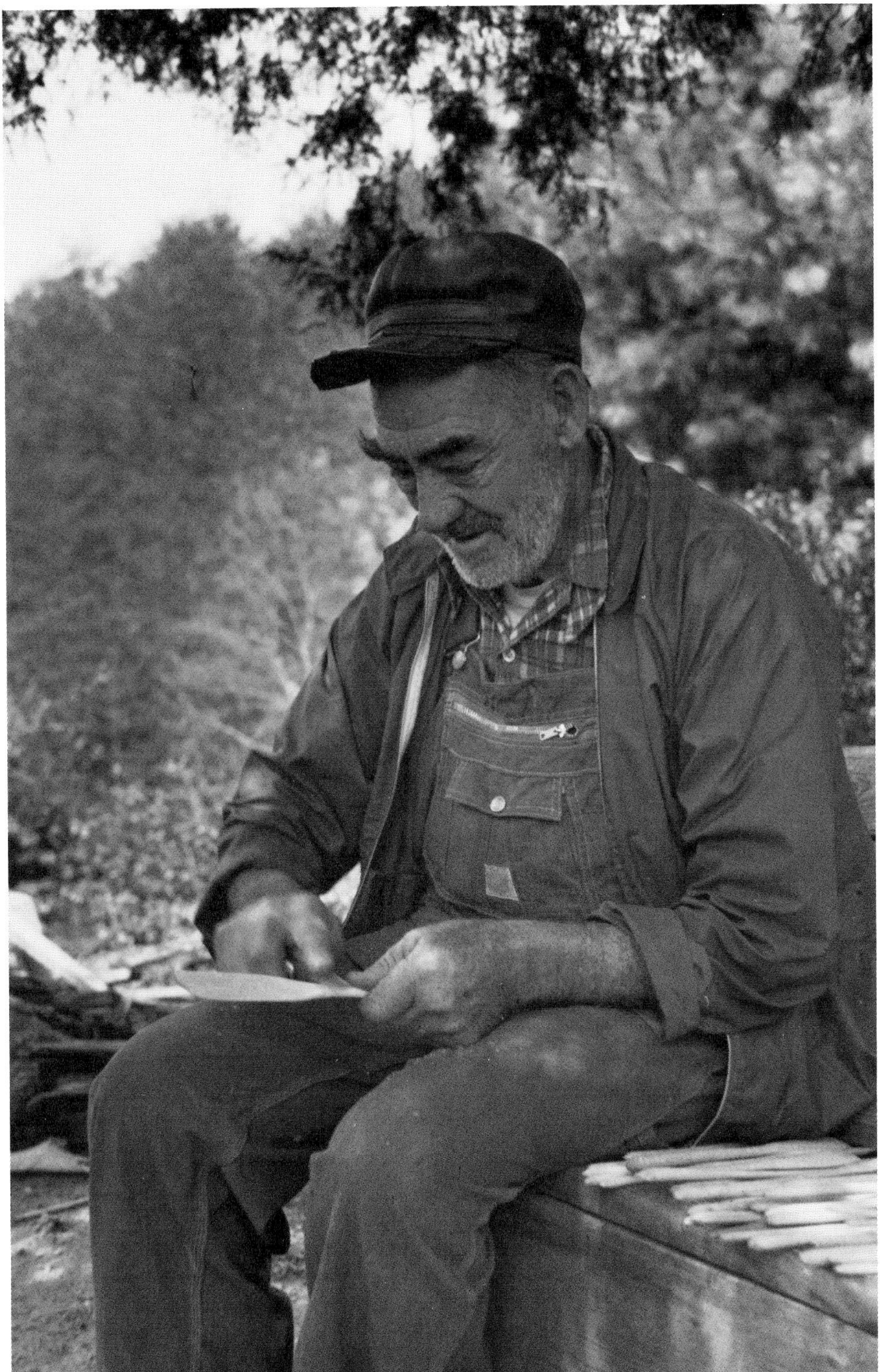

Summer

*My friend had a vineyard
  on a fertile hillside.
He dug the soil, cleared it of stones,
  and planted choice vines in it.*

Isaiah 5:1b-2

The patch is in a good spot; the soil is strong; it's sunny there much of the day. And when we get enough water, you've never seen so many beans. They say Ginny has a green thumb. It's true, but there's more to it than thumbs. The land itself has a lot to do with it. The land requires some mothering, of course; but nature takes over and the vines are full before you know it. And if picked often, they keep bearing beans right up until the frost.

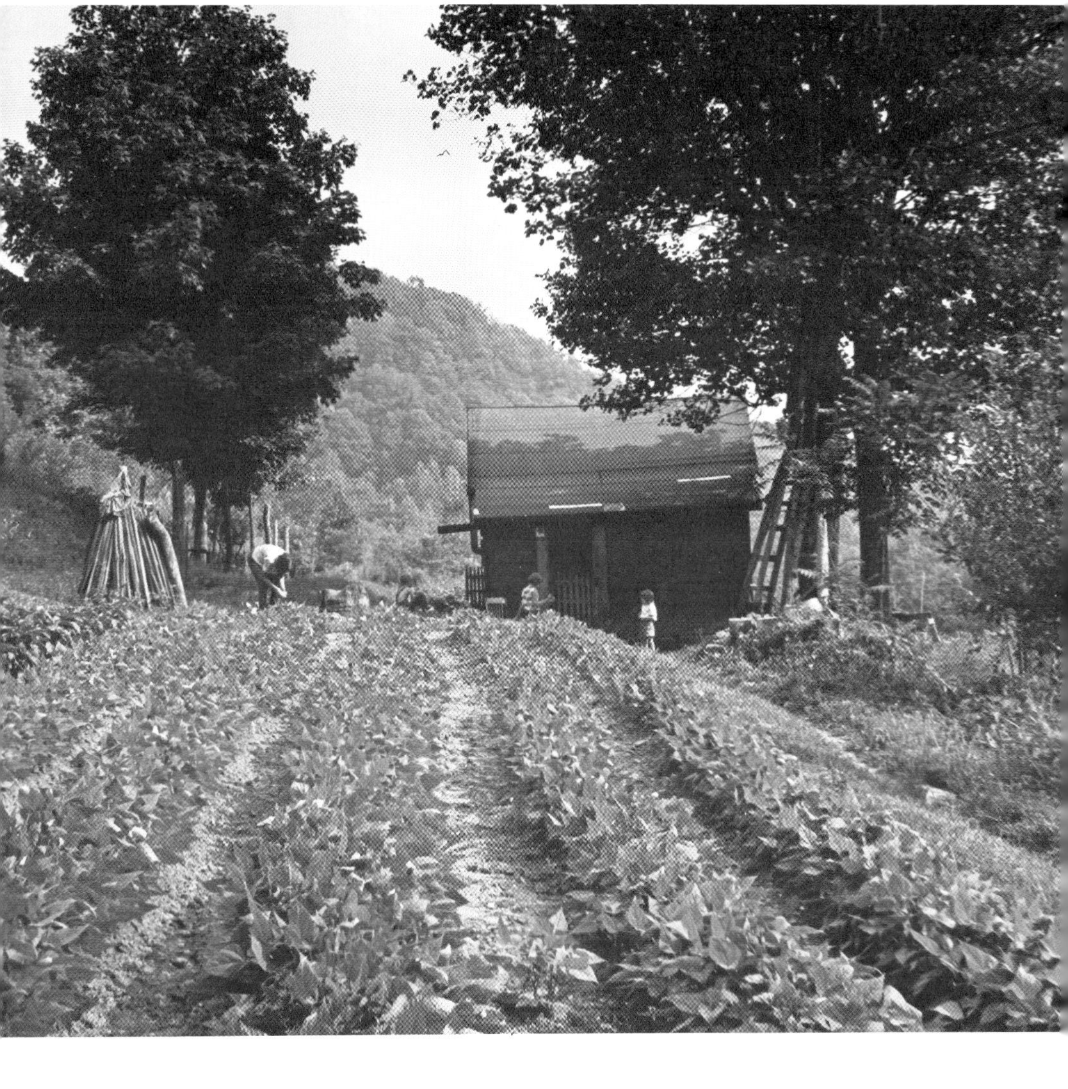

Summer

"*House of Israel, can not I do to you what this potter does?—it is Yahweh who speaks. Yes, as the clay is in the potter's hand, so you are in mine, House of Israel.*"

Jeremiah 18:6

We dare to touch the earth, to form it, to make mistakes with it. The earth does not resist the human hand. It accepts its shape, its destiny, its usefulness. It even touches us in return. Are we ourselves as free, as malleable as the earth, as open to becoming something new?

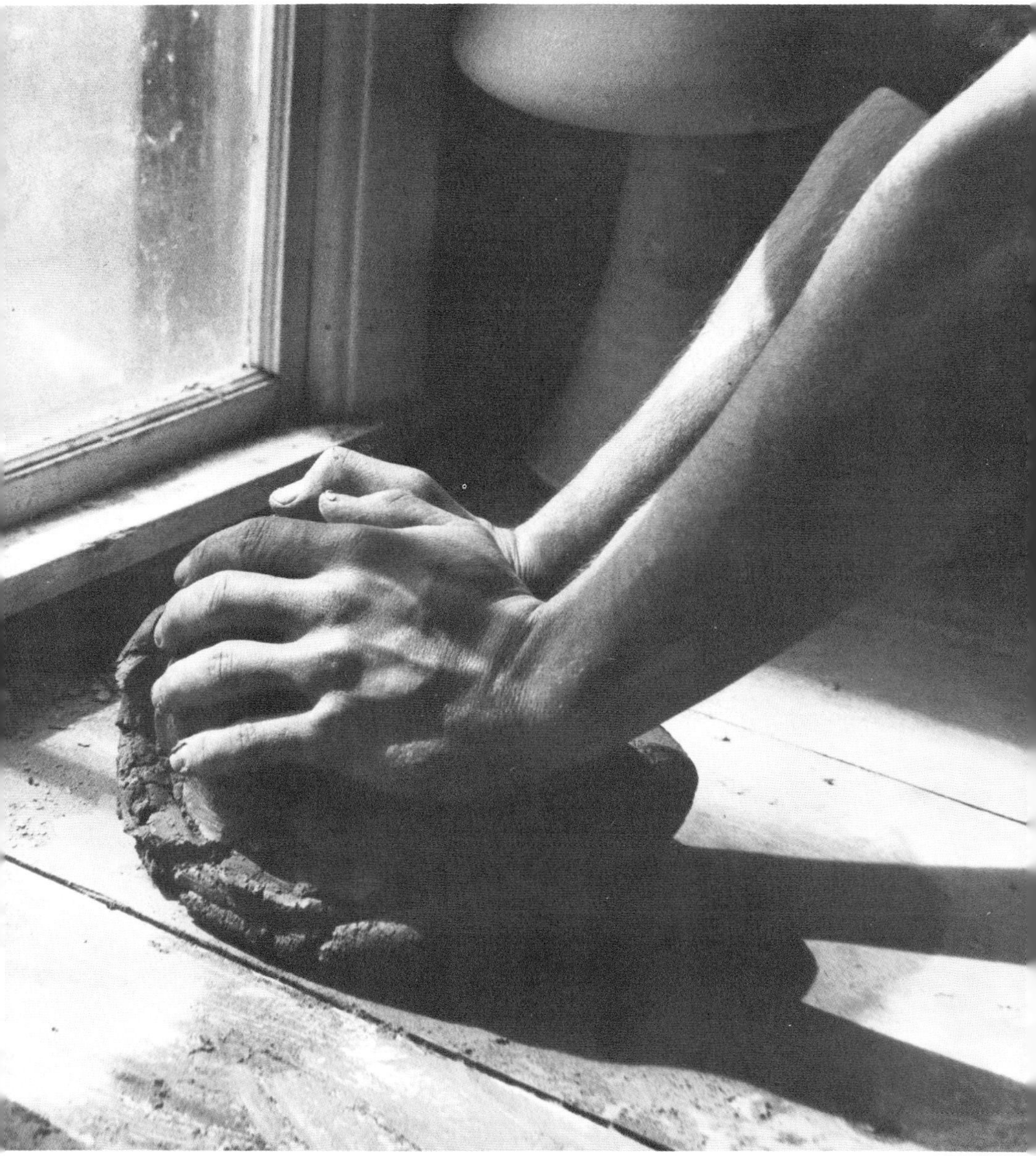

Summer

(Jesus) led them up a high mountain where they could be alone. There in their presence he was transfigured . . .

Matthew 17:1-2

We all need our consolation. The glory of what is to come has got to shine through on some occasion or through someone, or we'll get pretty low. We may climb a distant mountain to find the strength to carry on. We may even meet some fine folks living on the top of the mountain. Like Uncle Ben with his scythe. He always said, "I worked hard all my life. I never had to resort to preaching or to making moonshine."

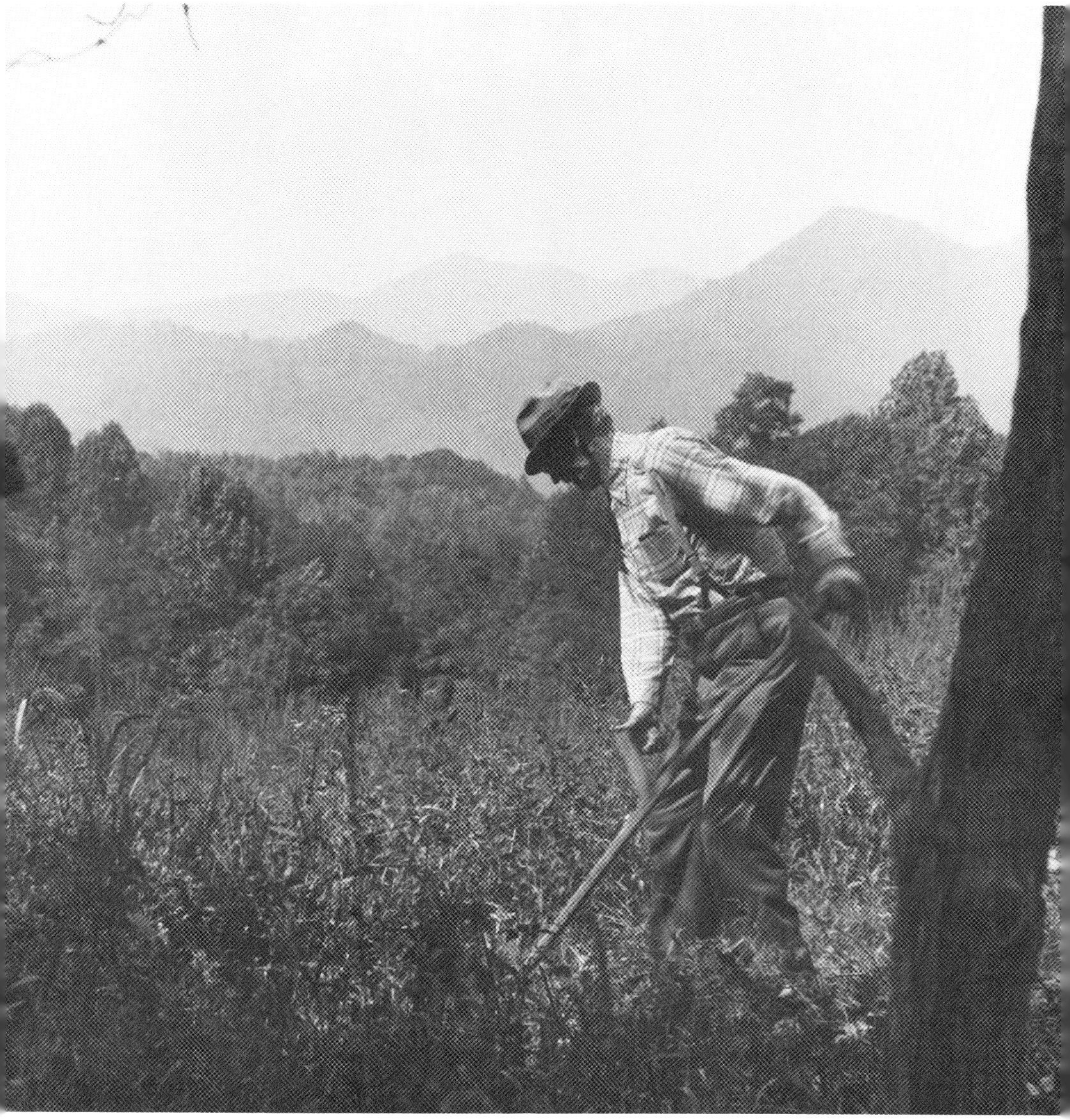

Summer

. . . and to guide our feet into the way of peace.

> Luke 1:79

    They just don't have to take another step today. Who'll try to stop them from swaying gently with the rocker, as I swat flies and fan my face. If they've got to move, they won't be very peaceable. I accept them, being a little scuffed from rocky roads, a bit worn and bulging at different spots. Am I talking about my shoes or my feet? They've been together so long they look alike.

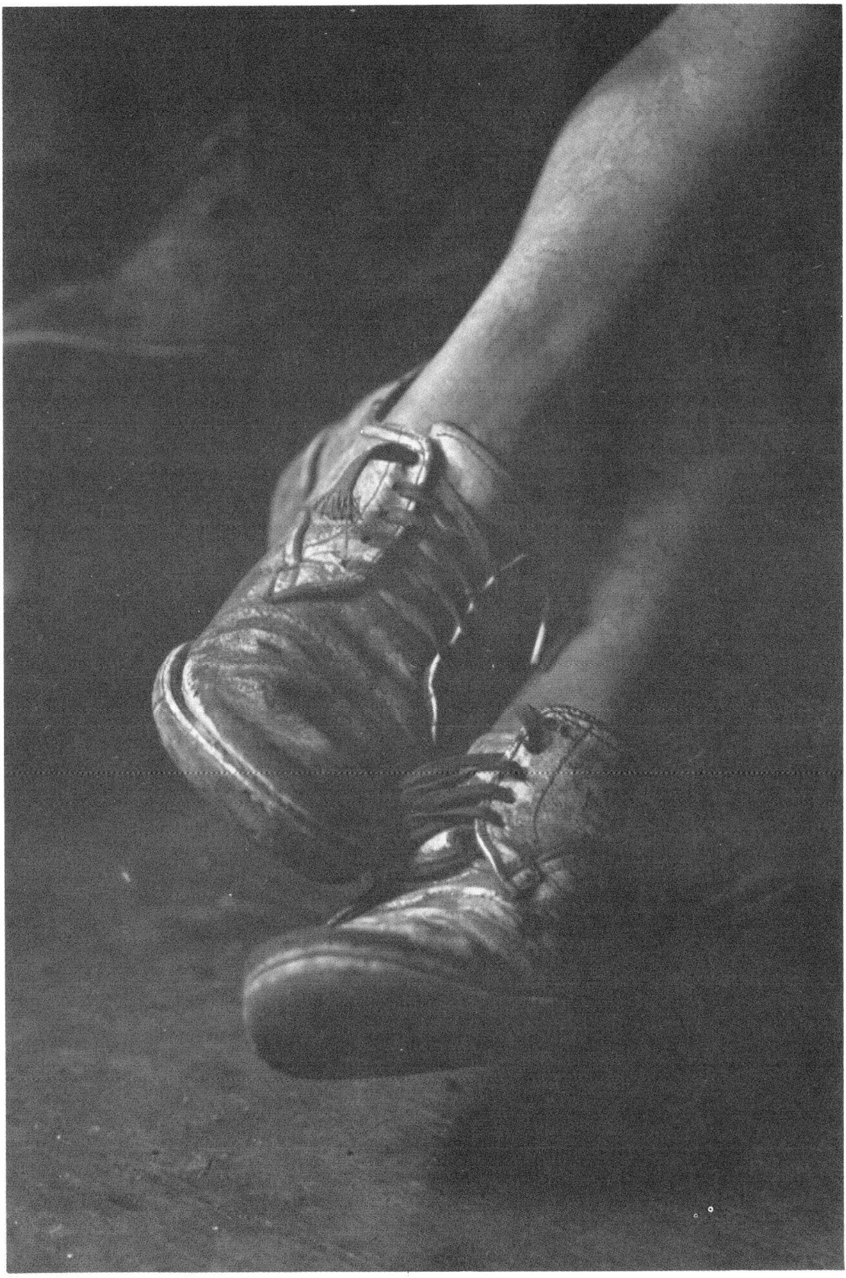

Summer

Meanwhile, let us go forward on the road that has brought us to where we are.

Philippians 3:16

We're not perfect, because we're out on the road as pilgrims. We've still got a lot of traveling and working and loving and coming together to do. The hills are raw and unfinished, and so are we. We have our bits of hatred, our clannishness, but we know they aren't right. Maybe in the Lord's good time we will be better.

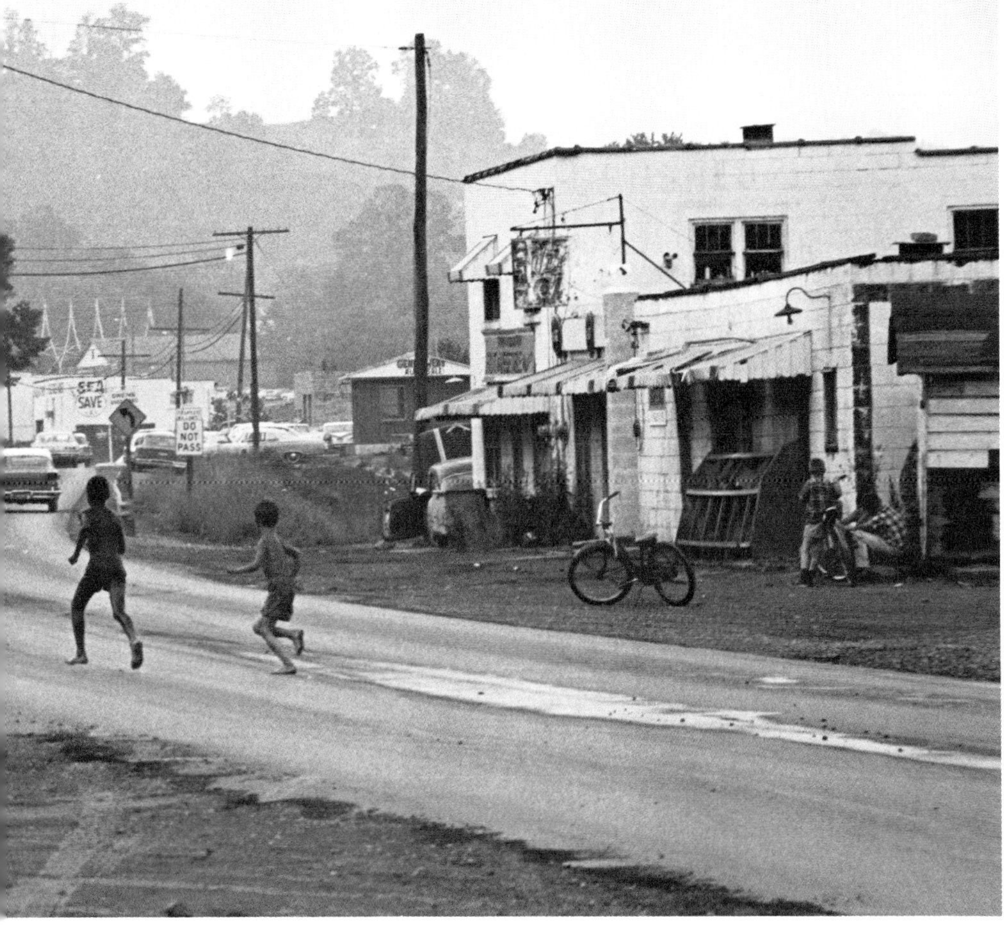
SAVE
DO
NOT
PASS

Summer

May our barns overflow with every possible crop . . .
         Psalm 144:13

      The land trusts that the rain will come and help it yield the bounty. We dwellers on the land are also confident that soil, rain, and weather will be just right. We trust together. The barn, shed, crib, and root cellar are ready for hay, tobacco, corn, and potatoes. We sharpen up the cutting tools and oil the machines for harvesting. We are all prepared, and now we must wait in hope.

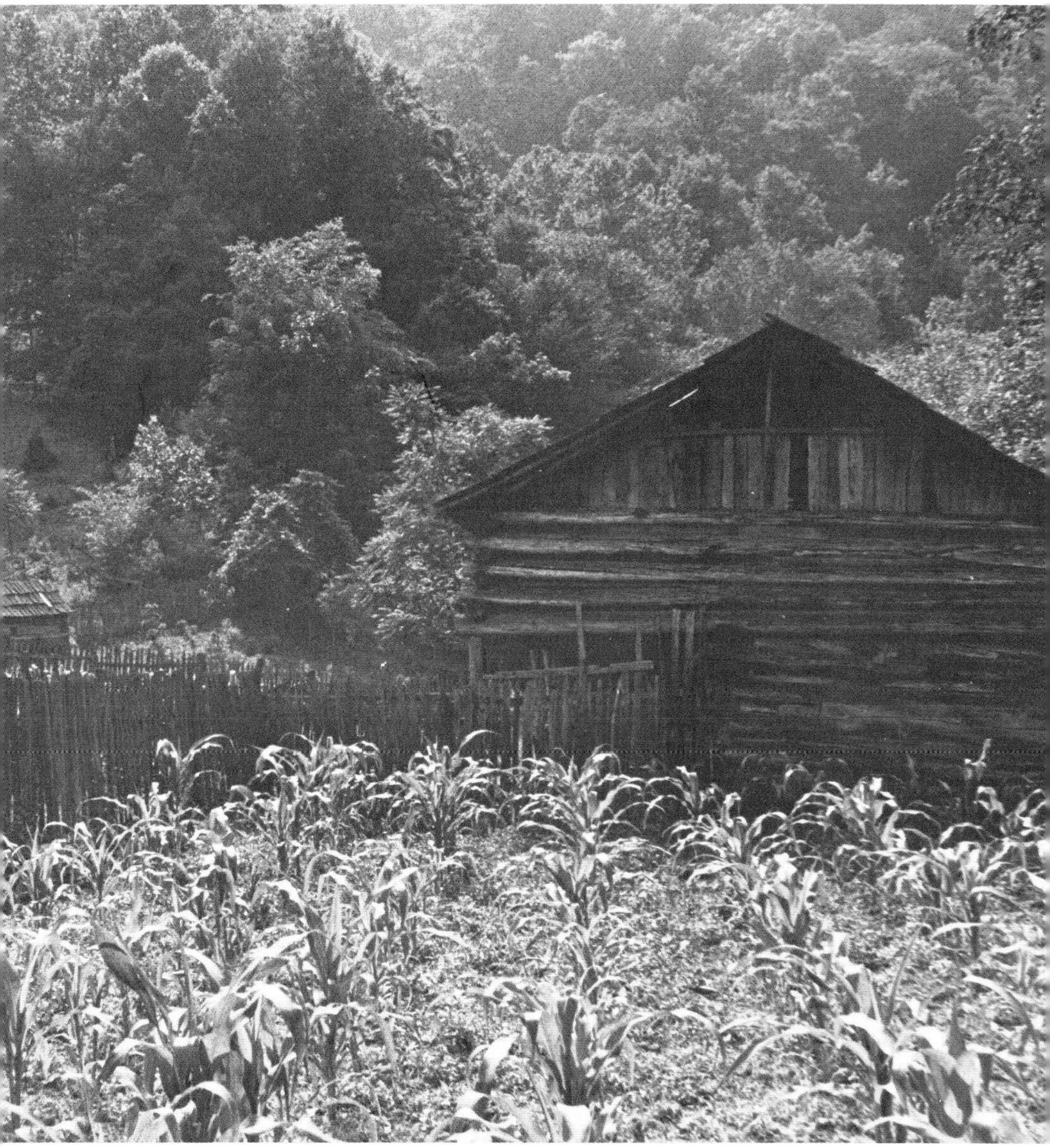

Summer

You must not muzzle an ox when it is treading out the corn.
                    Deuteronomy 25:4

      Each one knows when and where to find rest. Daddy told us how he took ole' Babe back over the road along which she used to haul the goods from his homeplace on the hill to our farm. The old horse stopped dead still at the exact spot where the team always rested some twenty years before, but now she had no load. The place must have been embedded in her brain. Daddy couldn't budge her until the time had passed that it would have taken to refresh the sweaty team. Would that we could recognize our own need for rest so well.

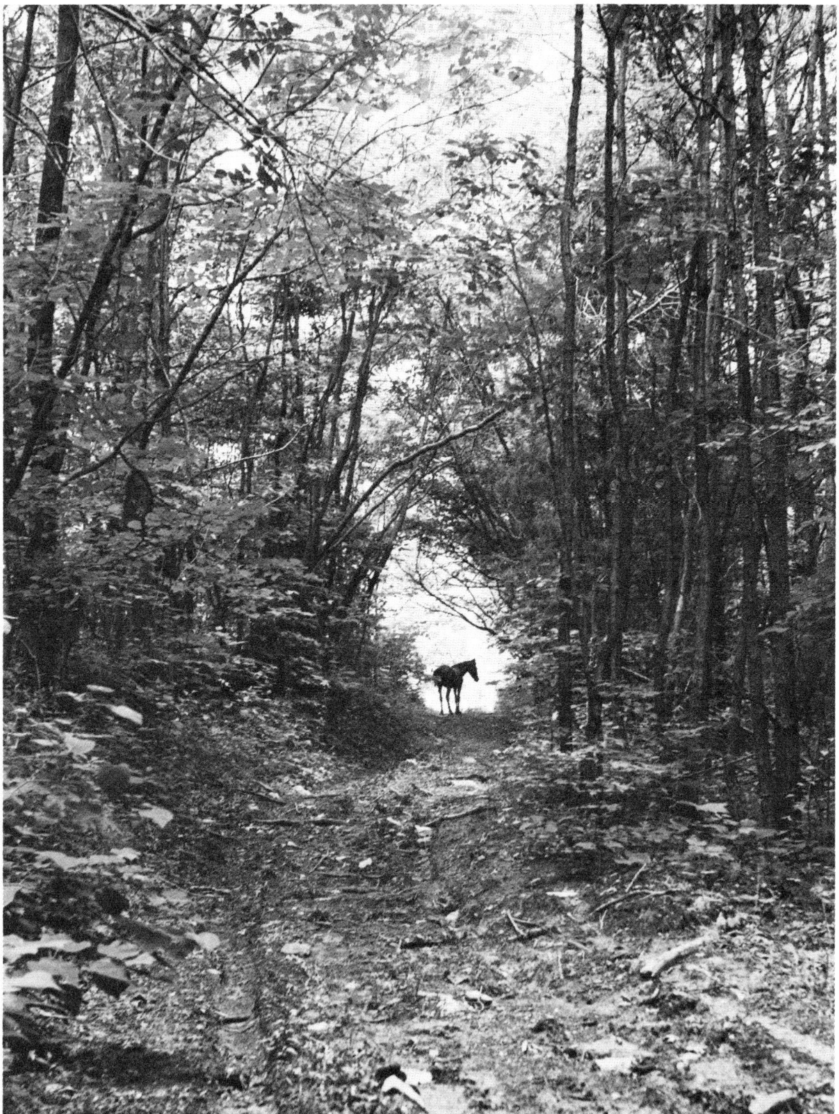

Summer

*To your brother say, "People of mine,"
to your sister, "Beloved."*

                      Hosea 3:5-6

    Crude spans, so they are; but they break the isolation of our people and bring the holler folks a little closer to everybody else.
   Crude, you say. It takes a feat of mind and hand to build with nothing, to arch the flood, to bear the load, and to stay the years.

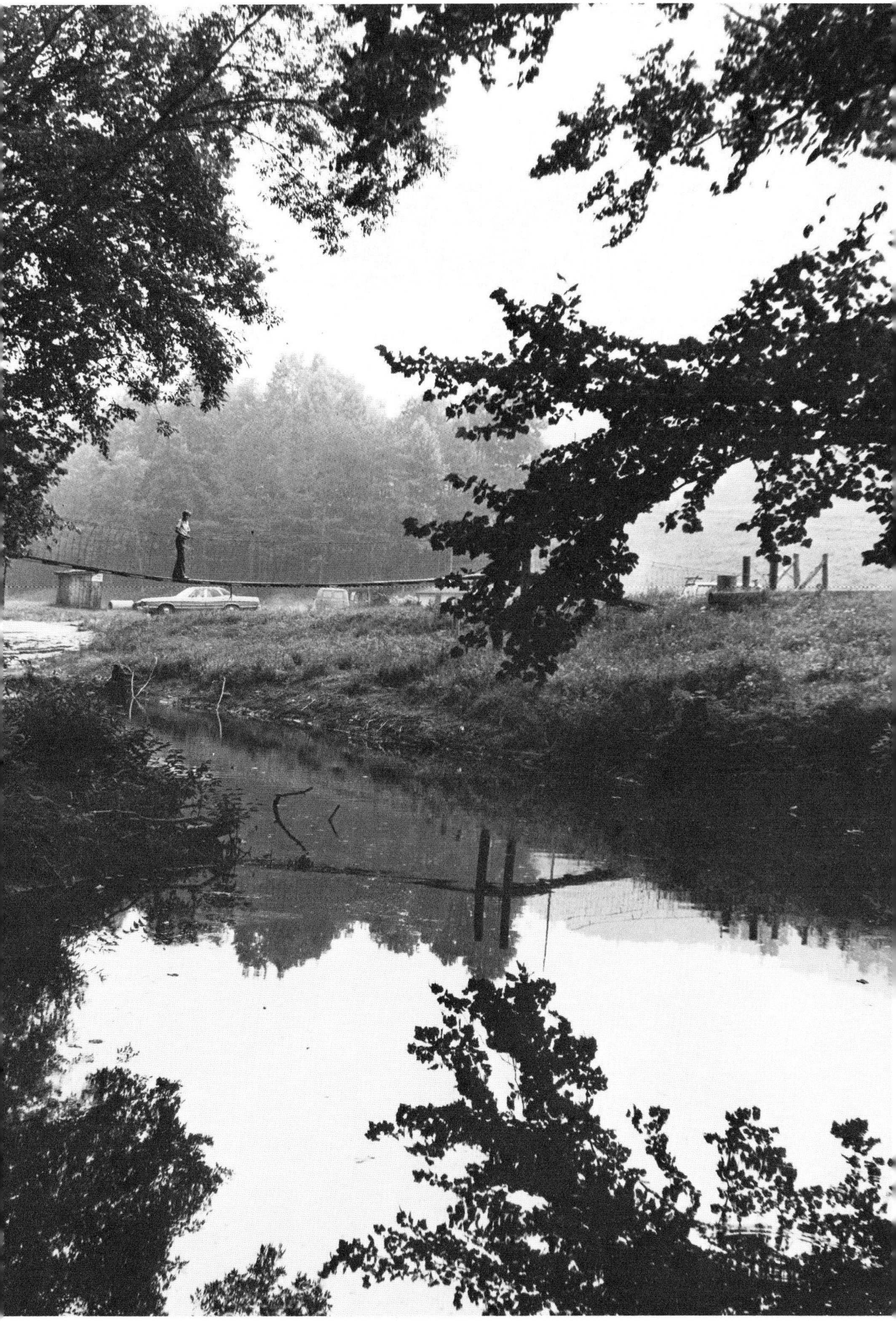

Summer

He brought us here and gave us this land, a land where milk and honey flow.
					Deuteronomy 26:9

Dear Aunt Mary,

    We stopped by Cedar Cliff Lake on our way west today. The trees on the shore, the cloudless sky, the shimmering water were all so beautiful. Sights blended with the sounds of katydids, distant crows, and water lapping on the rocks. We could smell the pine oil and the fragrances of flowers and life itself. I didn't taste the water, but the entire earth was sweet like honey. The folks almost drove away without me.

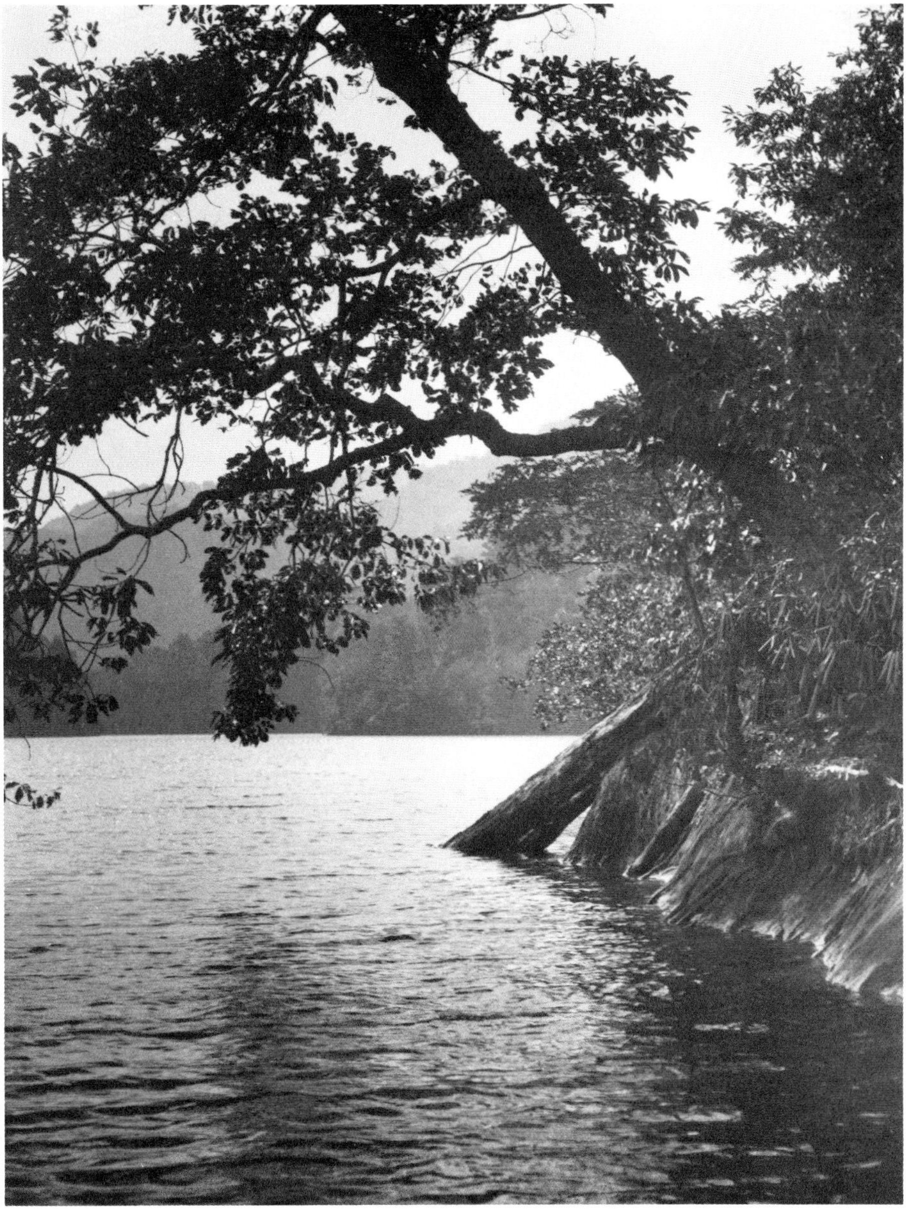

Summer

I will bring them back to the very soil I gave their ancestors.

Jeremiah 16:15

Every time we went to visit the homeplace, I went off alone. I couldn't help but scratch in the dirt and think of my grandfolks. They liked this land and worked it well with their hands and hoes. With our tractors work is easier, but are we better off? Gas is high, and a tractor costs so much more than a hoe. We could get back to just scratching for a living—but would we do it? Yet we must not forget our past. There's too much of our grandfolks' sweat still left in this dust.

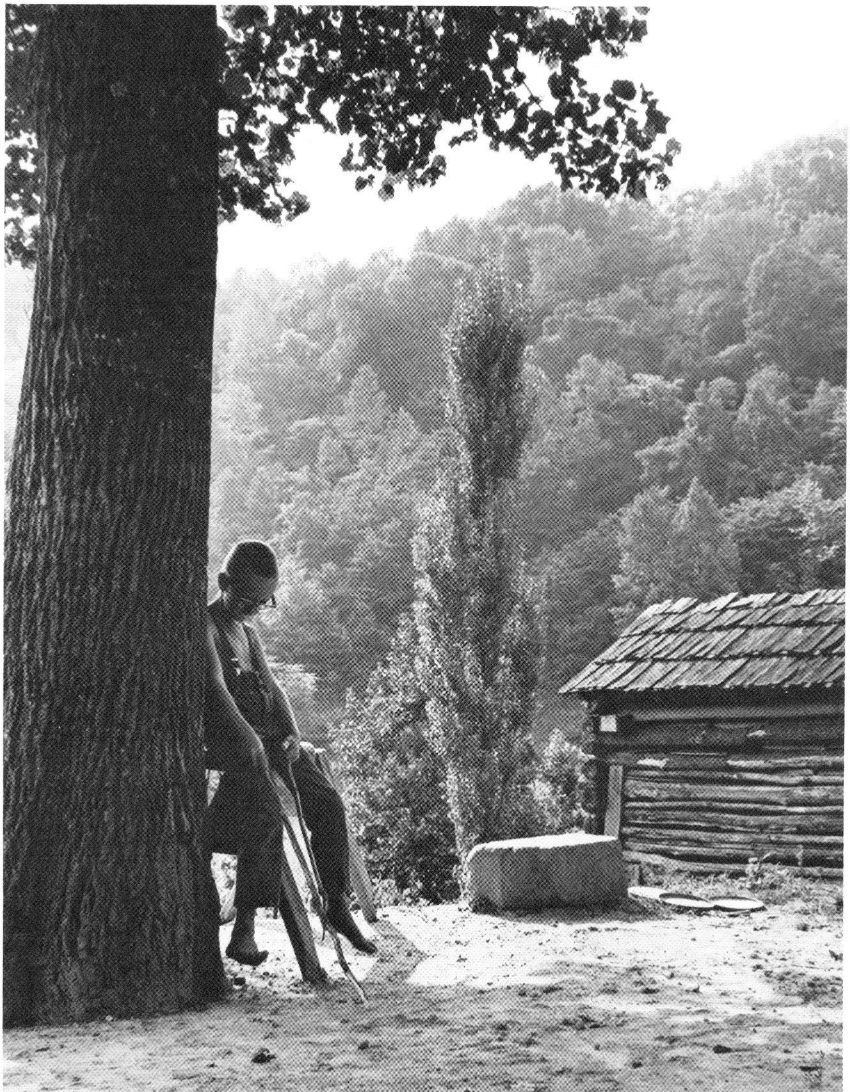

Summer

*Do all you can to preserve the unity of
  the Spirit
by the peace that binds you together.*
                    Ephesians 4:3

They always worked out the verses together. He could hardly see anymore, and she had good eyes but not the wisdom of the years. They seemed to grow together, the one young, the other old. Each needed the other. Such sharing is the glue that binds folks together, that makes communities live and grow. Maybe other parts of the nation need Appalachia, just as we need them. We're not a basket case; we've also got something to give.

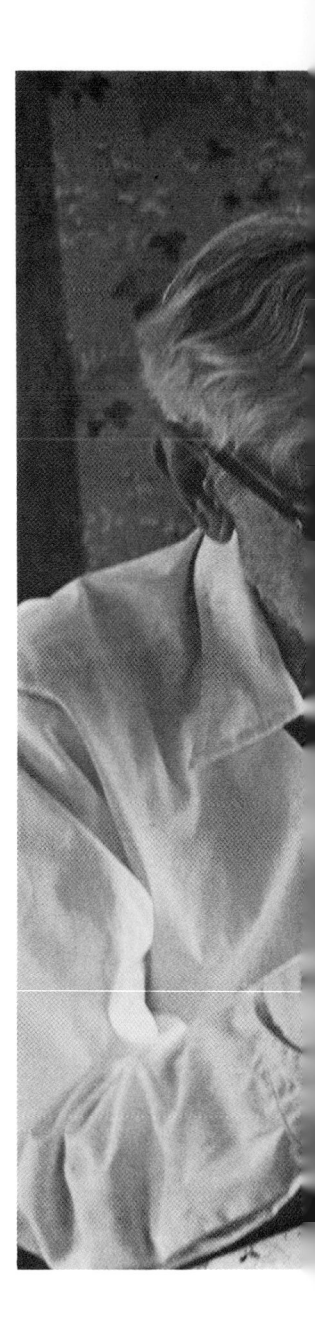

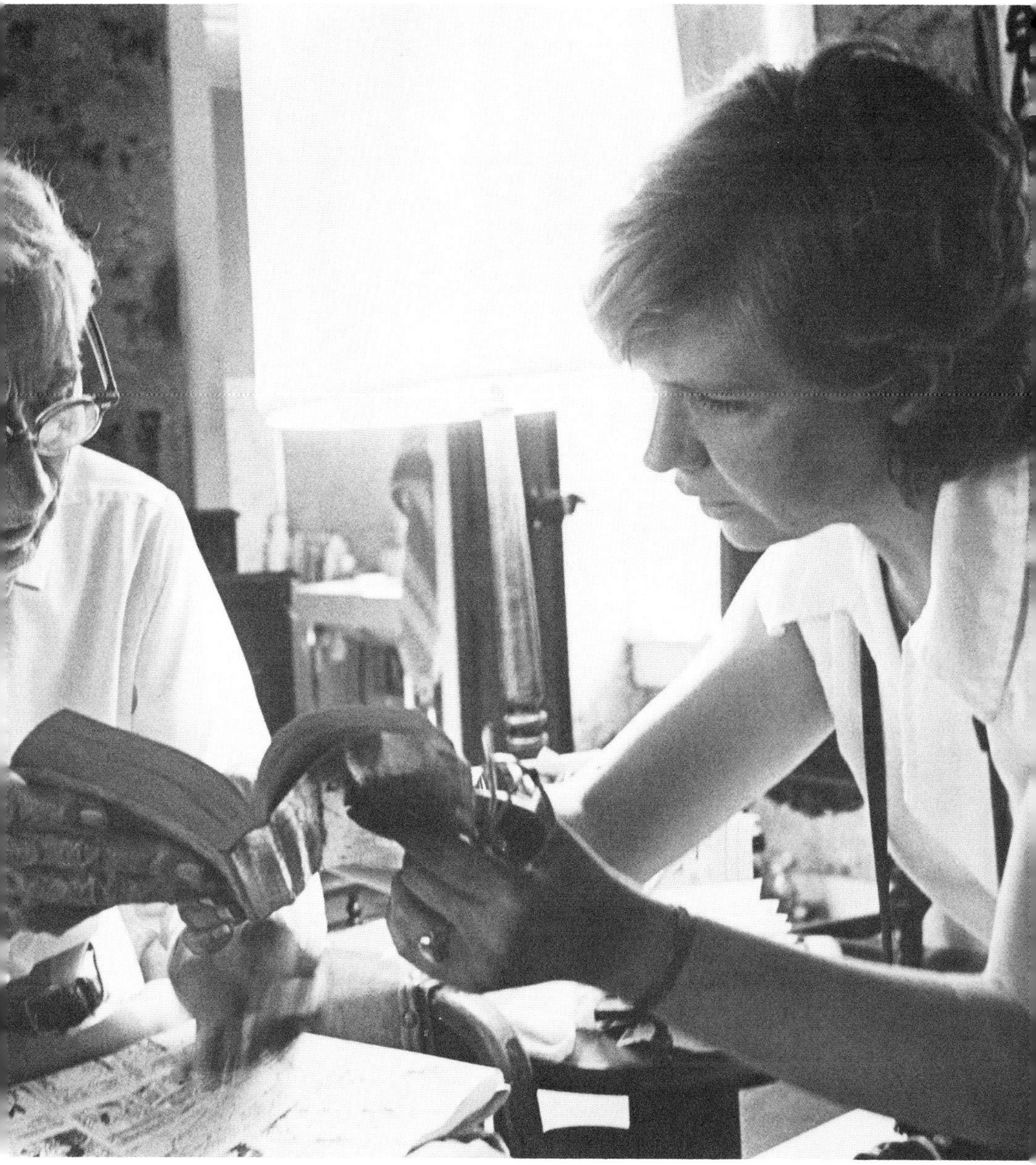

Summer

> *When you see a cloud looming up in the west you say at once that rain is coming, and so it does. And when the wind is from the south you say it will be hot, and it is.*
>
> Luke 12:54-55

    We know some of the signs of our earth, but not all of them. Animals speak to us in various ways, and we must be open to their signs as well. Some just want to show affection and wag their tails or lick our face. Having such creatures around makes us know we are worth loving after all.

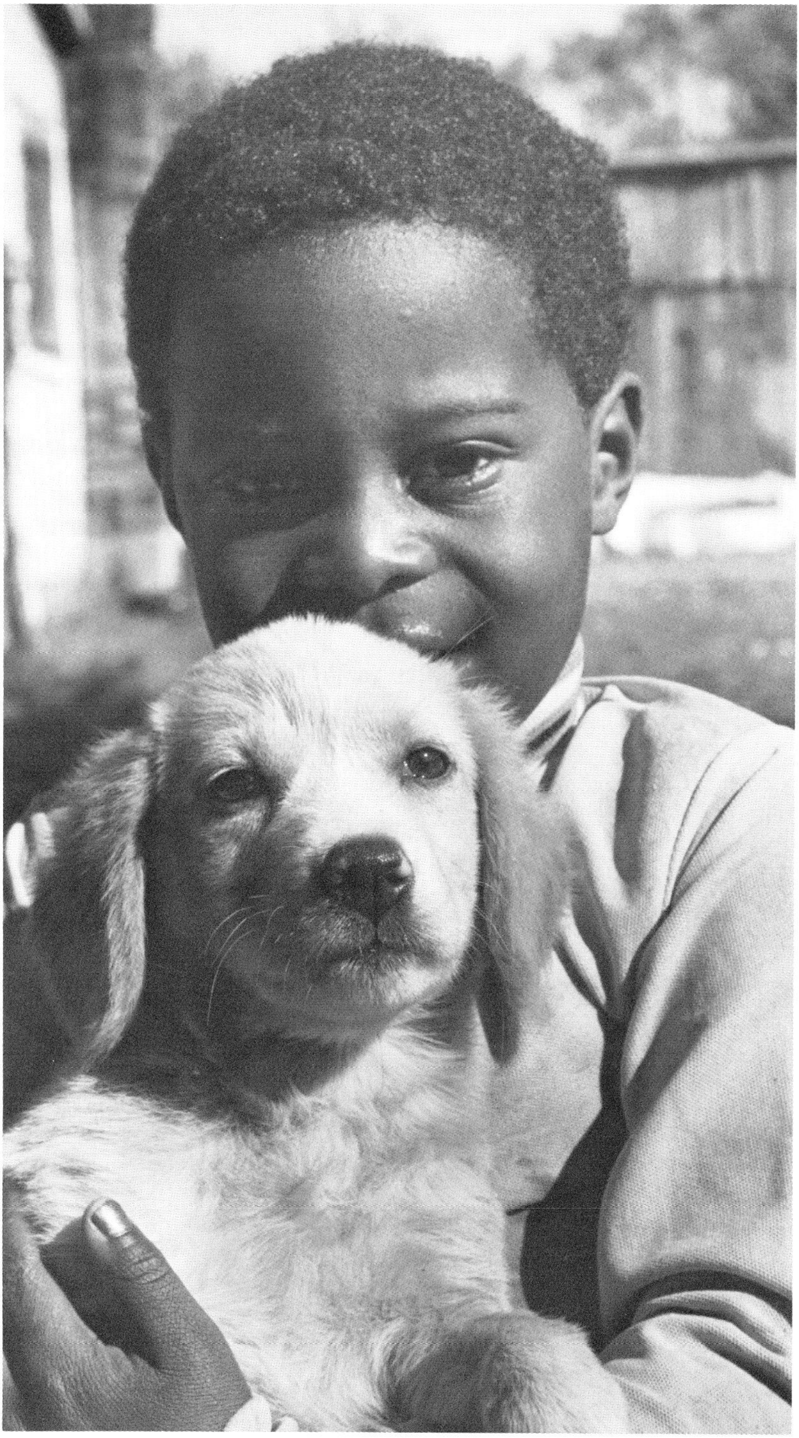

Summer

. . . as soon as its twigs grow supple and its leaves come out, you know that summer is near. So with you when you see all these things: know that he is near, at the very gates.

Matthew 24:32-33

    So many things stand in the way. We busy ourselves building the distractions that snare others. We have to look around them to discover the true signs of the times, which show themselves readily to those with open minds and hearts. Chart the changes of the season, the day the birds come back, the week the buds appear. Be enchanted by nature's call, which asks us neither to buy or sell, to trade or keep.

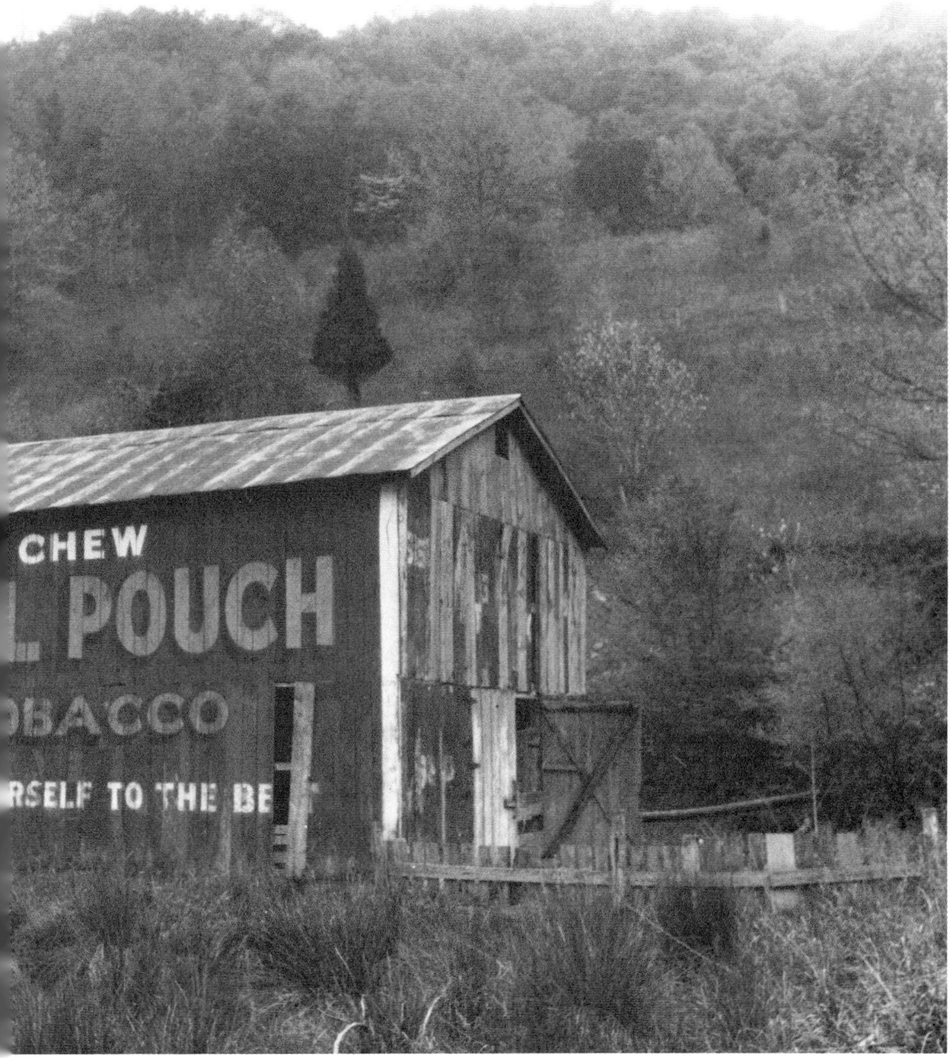
CHEW
POUCH
TO THE

Autumn

Autumn

> *Deposit generosity in your storerooms and it will release you from every misfortune.*
>
> Ecclesiasticus 29:15

The squirrels know the time of year; so do the ants, the bees, and almost all human beings. Fall is in the smell of the air and the ache of the bones. It's time to clean the chimney, put away the screens, clear out the attic, fill up the cord wood bin, and lay away provisions for winter. The season's going to be busy. The wildlife seem to be telling us something.

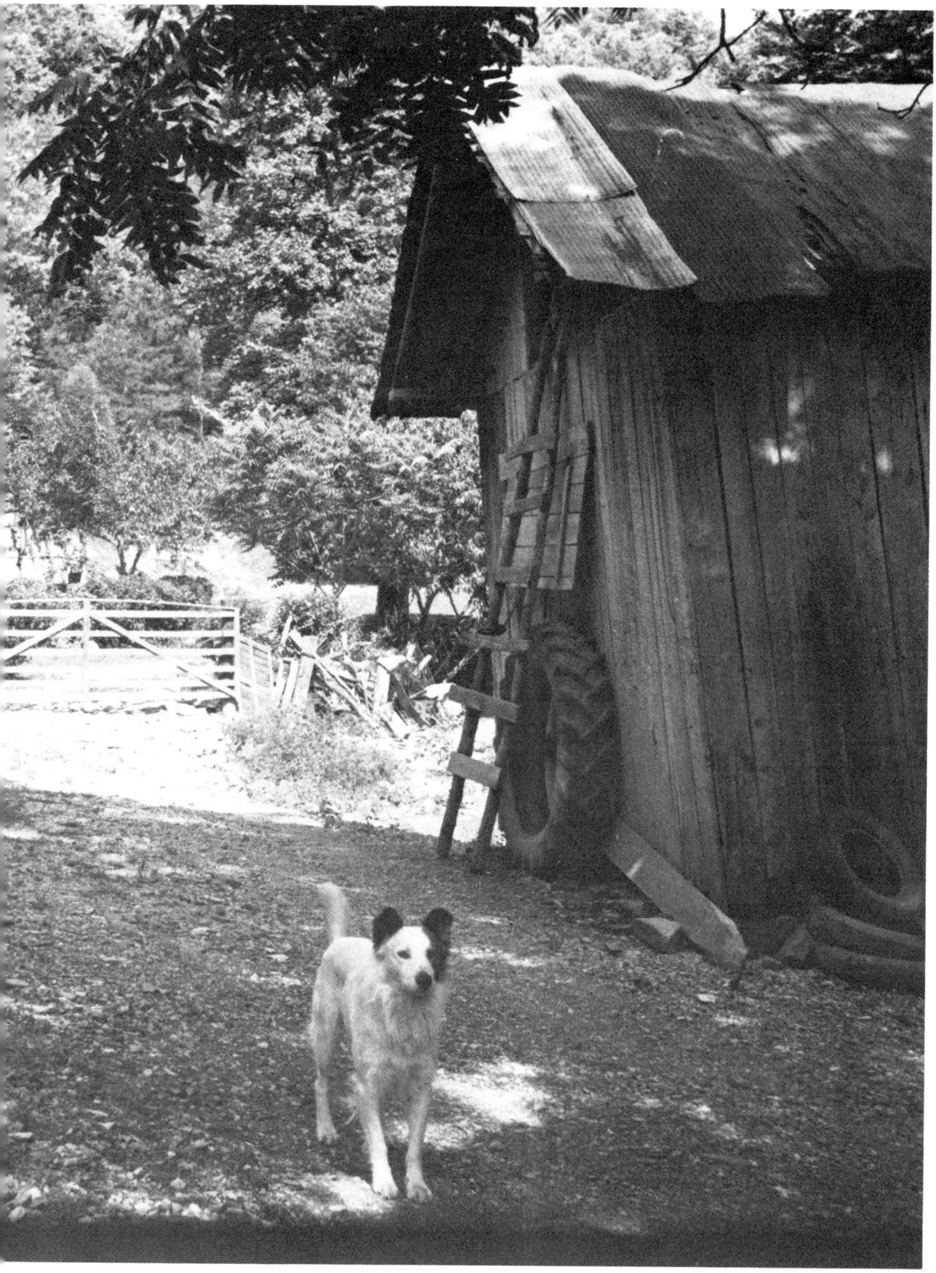

Autumn

*You visit the earth and water it,
you load it with riches.*
                    Psalm 65:9

It's silent now. The kids have gone back to school; the old water hole has been repossessed by frogs and turtles. The growing season is ending, and leaves are in their last flush before they turn and fall. This is the season of bounty, the season to be thankful for good times and good crops. The pause after busy activity is part of the land's own rhythm.

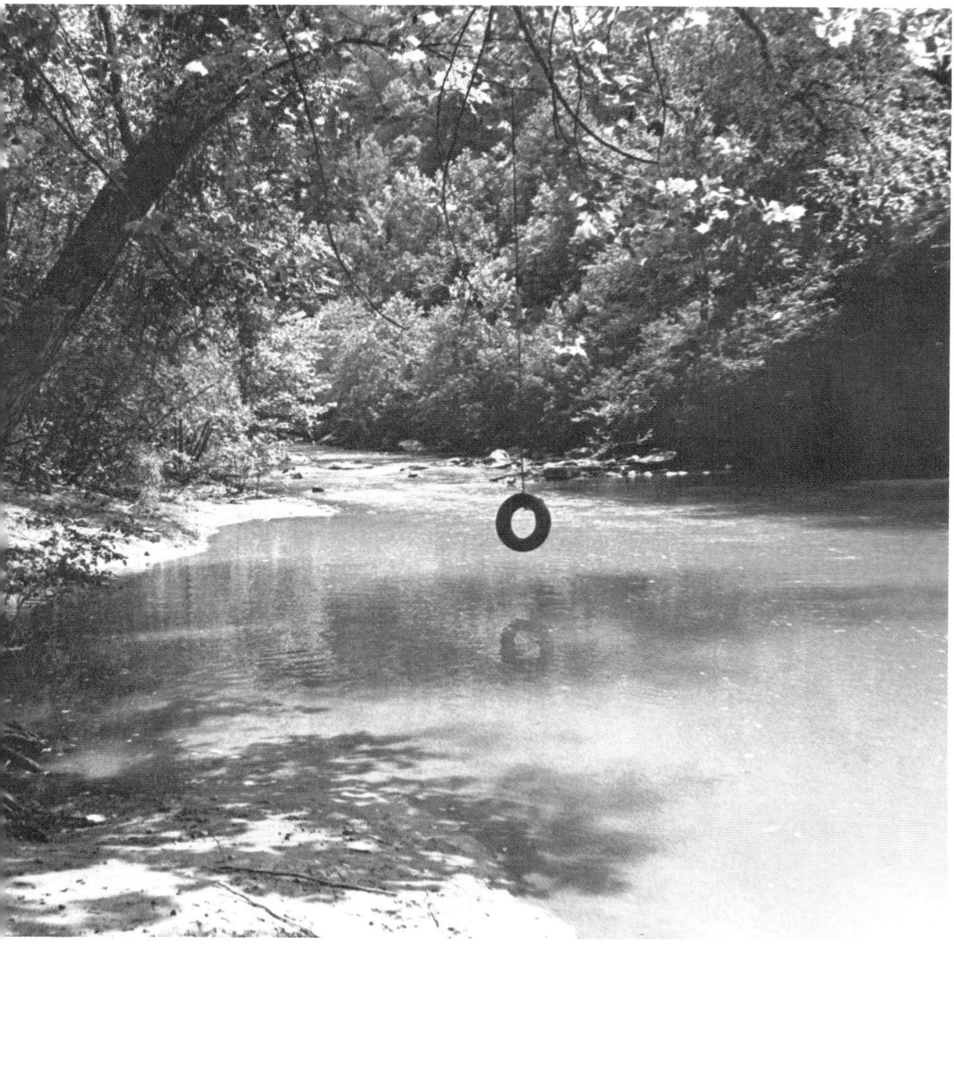

Autumn

"When reaping the harvest in your field, if you have overlooked a sheaf in that field, do not go back for it. Leave it for the stranger, the orphan and the widow, so that Yahweh your God may bless you in all your undertakings."
Deuteronomy 24:19

    We hang a few ears at the fireplace to remind ourselves that there has always been enough for us and plenty more besides for others. We can't be stingy. The Indian corn is a symbol of our Native American cultural forebearers. They showed us how to raise crops, share the harvest, and be thankful for what we have received.

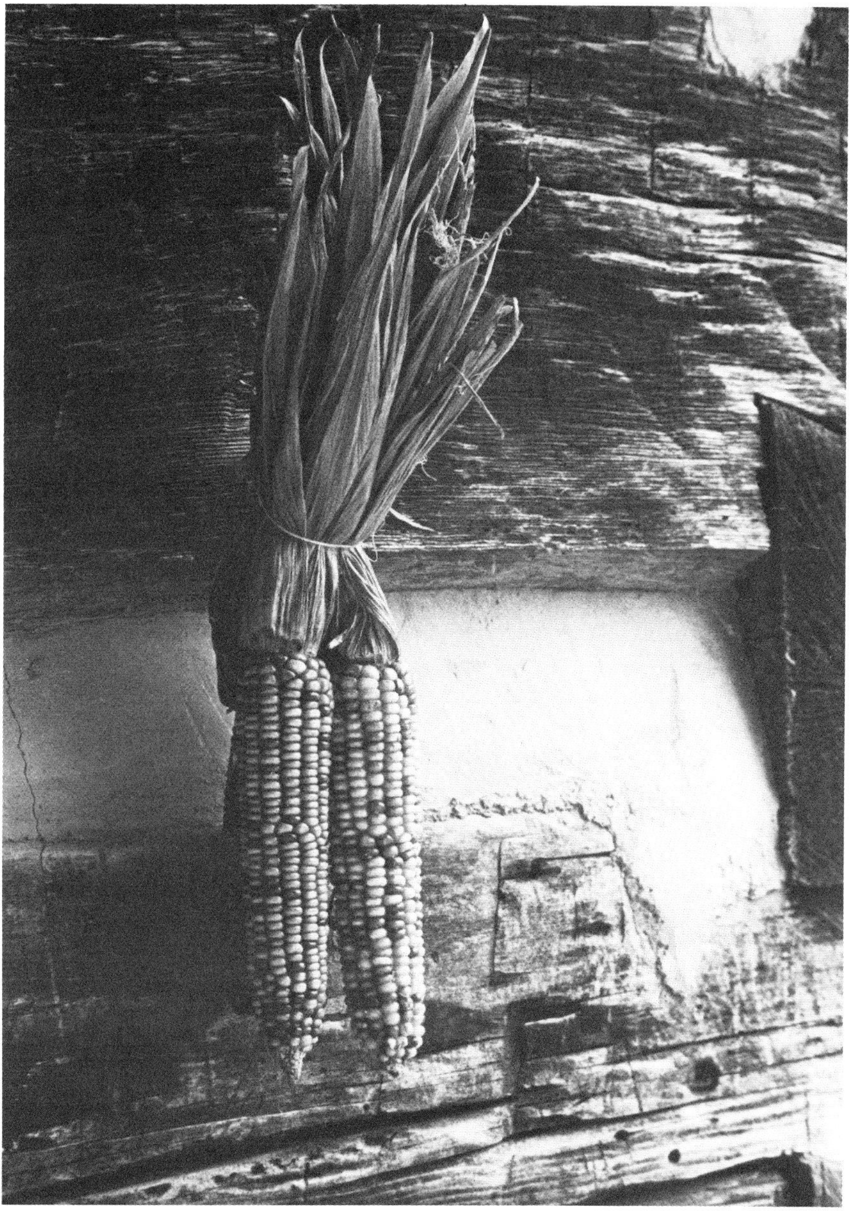

Autumn

He gave them so many days' determined time,
he gave them authority over everything on earth.

Ecclesiasticus 17:2-3

  Daddy's been gone now a number of years, but I choke up a little every time I return to the homeplace and enter our old smokehouse. The briny-hickory scent lingers amid the darkened crossbeams laced with meat-hooks and hanging wires. It's now a storage place, but then it was filled with the best of hams and shoulders and bacons. Daddy was the country curing king of Mason county, and few challenged that title in those parts. His smokehouse was his throne room, and there Daddy's spirit seems to hang around.

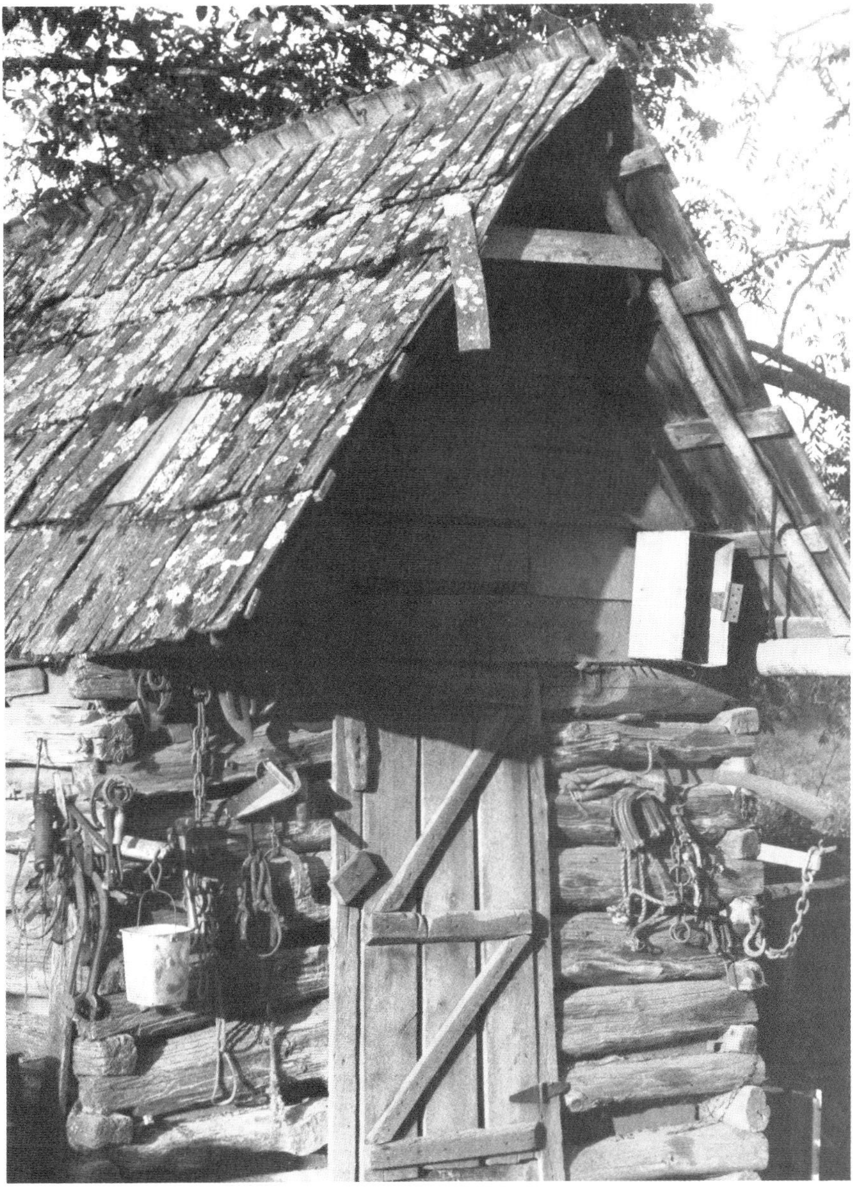

Autumn

*Mountains and hills! bless the Lord:
give glory and eternal praise to him.*

Daniel 3:75

    The grave site is soon healed and grass grows again. The one in the grave returns to dust. The stone weathers and crumbles in time. The last traces are soon gone. I remember as a boy coming across the remains of a slave cemetery hardly 120 years old. We returned years later and couldn't find it; it had disappeared—but what about the folks buried there? The tombstones testify to eternal rest for all who return to dust. Eternal means endless—and that is the heart of mountain faith.

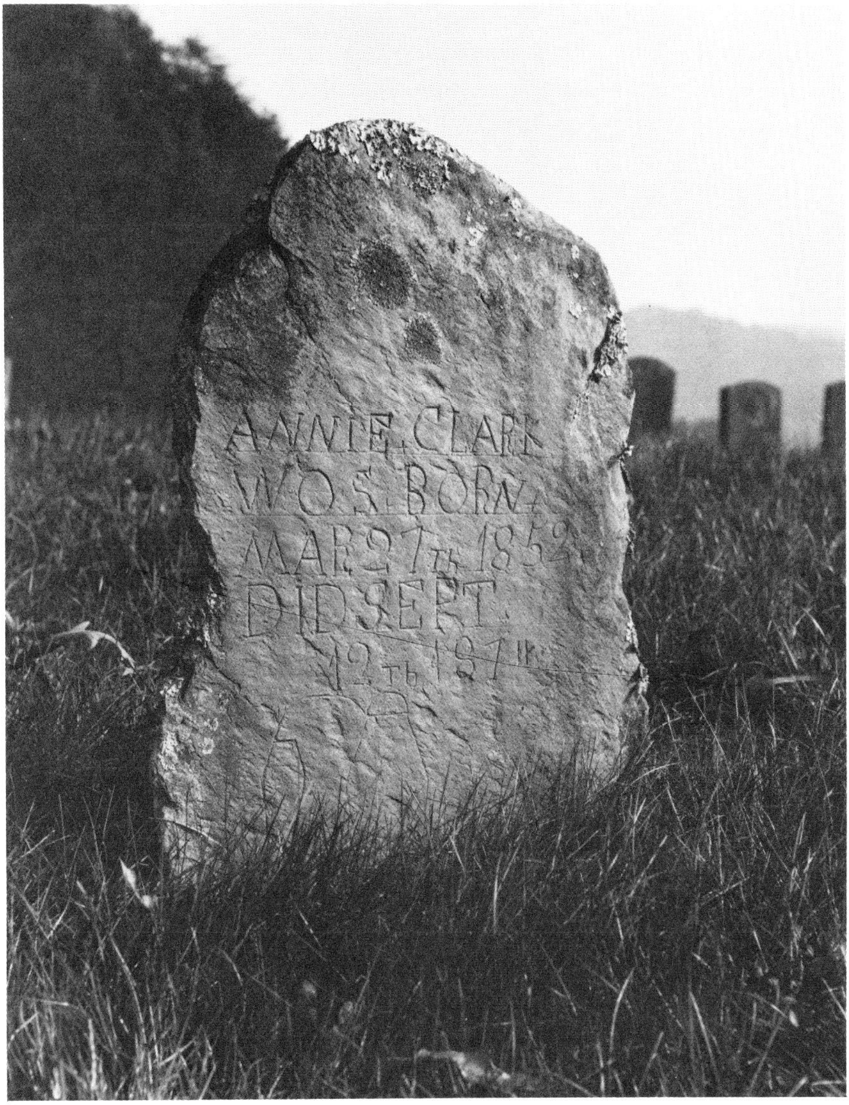
ANNIE CLARK
WOS BORN
MAR 27th 1852
DID SEPT
12th 1871

Autumn

There is a variety of gifts but always the same Spirit; there are all sorts of service to be done, but always the same Lord; working in all sorts of different ways in different people, it is the same God who is working in all of them.

1 Corinthians 12:4-6

Making good sorghum is more than an art; it's a community project. The master has to be gifted; but he doesn't do things by himself. You've got to have good growers, good harvesters, good fire-tenders, good skimmers, good bottlers. They all work to make the taste just right—and no one knows more about sorghum tasting than those who produce it. Even visitors are important. They add a little enthusiasm and excitement to otherwise pretty hard work.

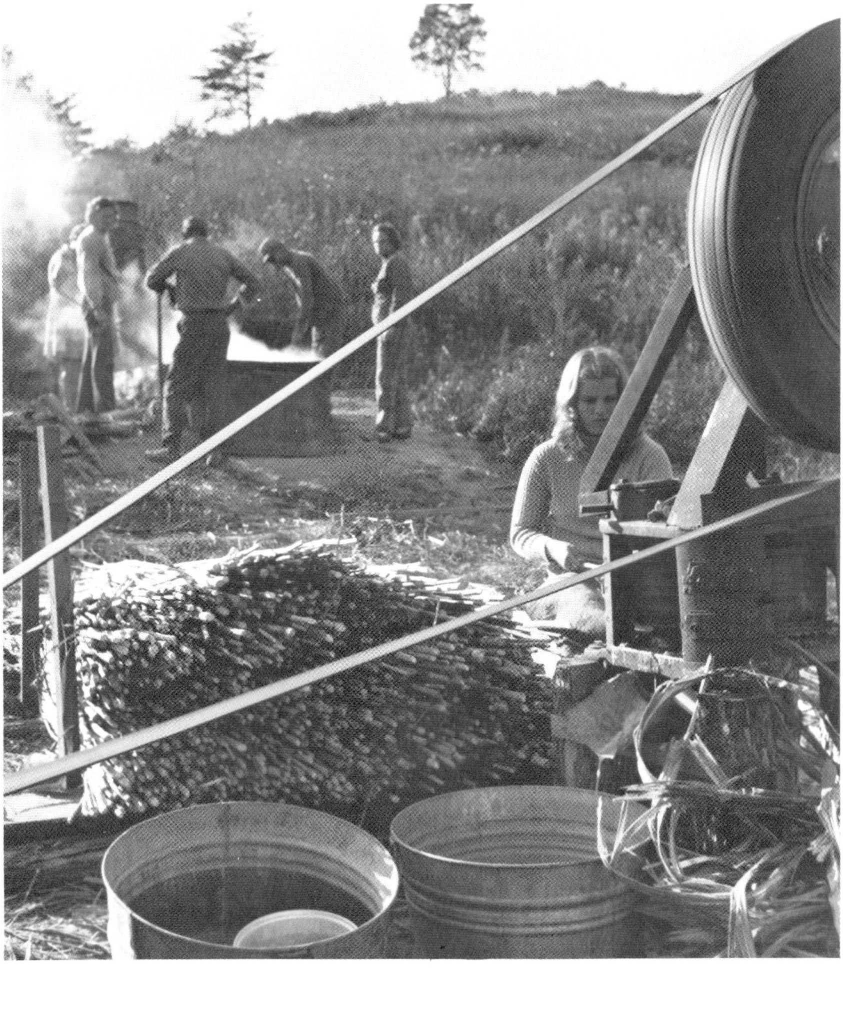

Autumn

There is a season for everything . . .
  A time for searching,
  a time for losing,
  a time for keeping,
  a time for throwing away.
  Ecclesiastes 3:1,6

    Autumn's colors suggest mortality. Summer life is fading fast, the days are shorter, and nature itself seems to pause as though winded. The trees know all this and more besides. The leaves and sap and nuts fall. It's just that time. If trees know so well, why shouldn't we? Why should we strive for a youth that's past? It's time to take things slower, and to do so gracefully. In fact, we might start living in the October of our lives.

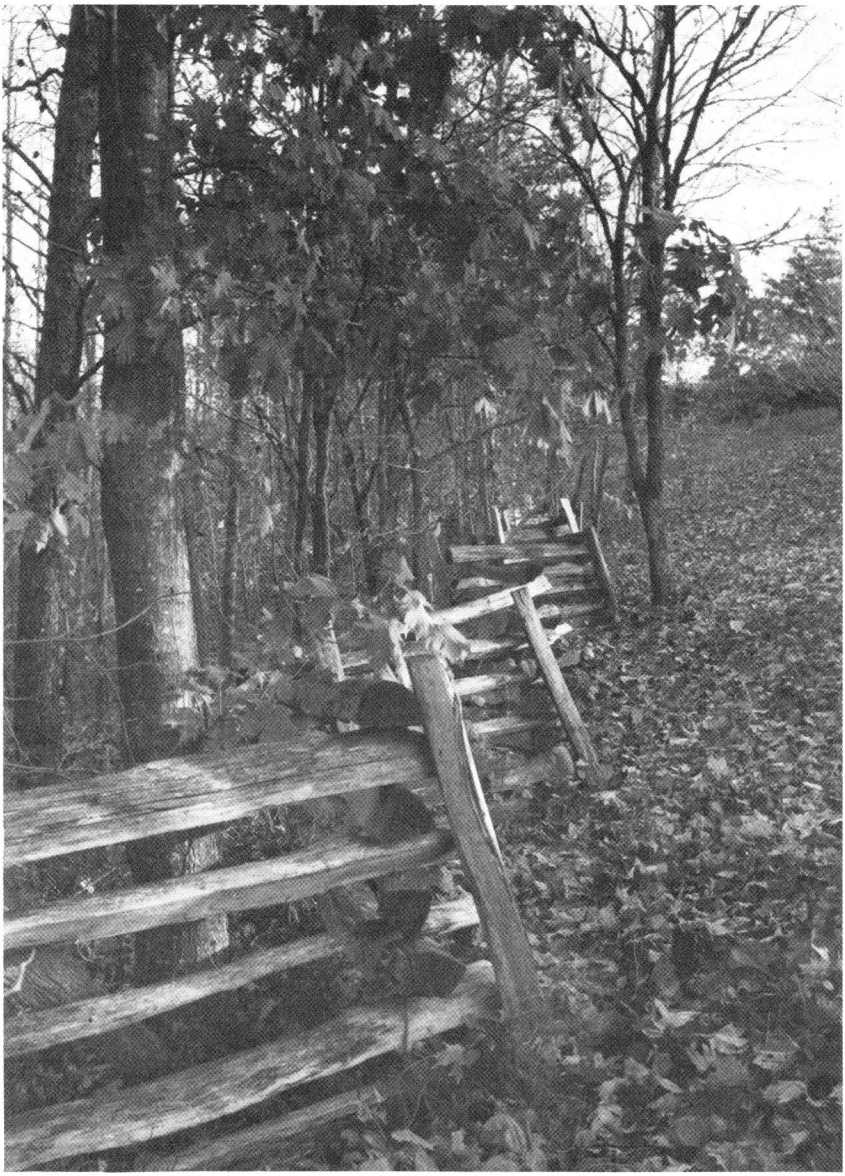

Autumn

*No longer are you to be named
 "Forsaken,"
nor your land "Abandoned,"
but you shall be called "My Delight,"
and your land "The Wedded";*
             Isaiah 62:4

      Land and people. So close that they look alike and act the same. Appalachia and Appalachians blend into one, drawn together by the beauty—the misty hills, the trees in brilliant color, the earth clouds along the river bottoms on chilly mornings. We are bound into a curtained wedding bed—and we can't escape.

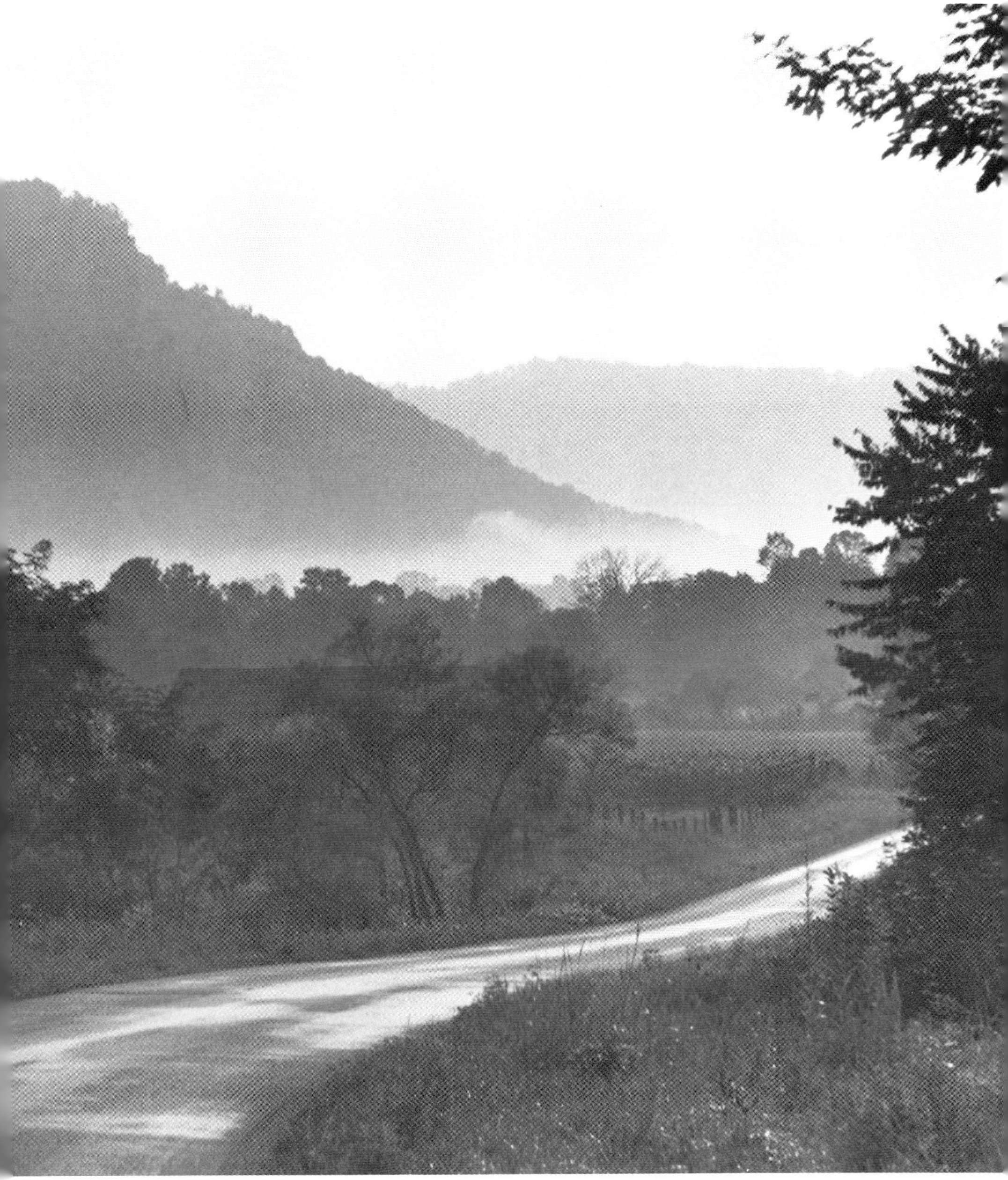

Autumn

*Open the gates of virtue to me,
  I will come in and give thanks to
  Yahweh.
This is Yahweh's gateway,
  through which the virtuous enter.*

Psalm 118:19-20

Human faults build fences, tall and unclimbable. All sinners wall themselves in, imprisoned by their own hands. Each needs a way out, a gate with well-oiled hinges and easy latches—a way to leave the prisons of the mind and heart. Thank God for mountain gaps and passes, for paths and roads, for coves and gorges and fords and smooth-flowing water. Thank God the sinner can still find these, among the shadows of a dying year—and through some new beginning go out to broader space.

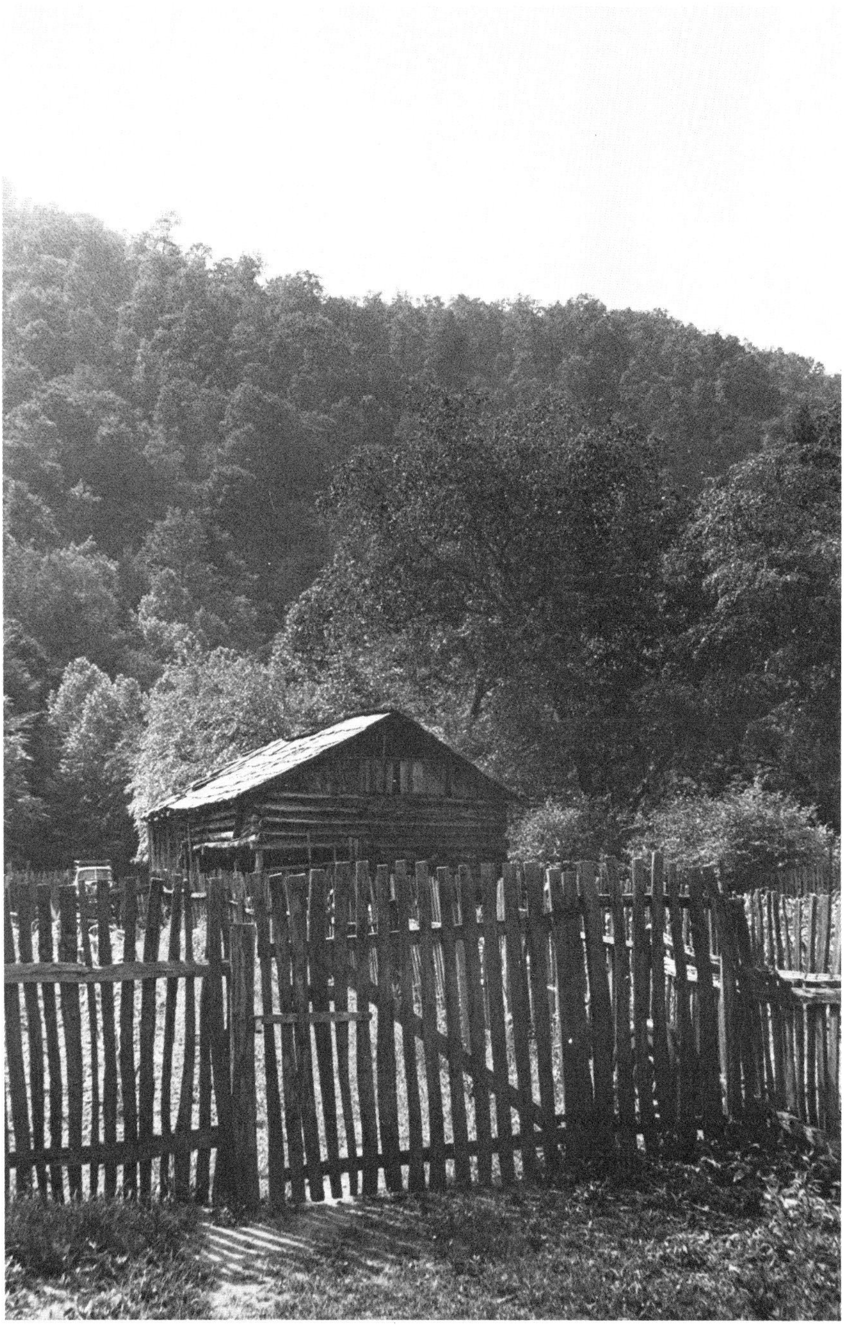

Autumn

*Look around you, look at the fields;
already they are white, ready for harvest!*
       John 4:35

  When they went to cut the grain, there was never enough time or hands or energy. The work had to be done, and the time was right. They always prayed to the Lord of the harvest.

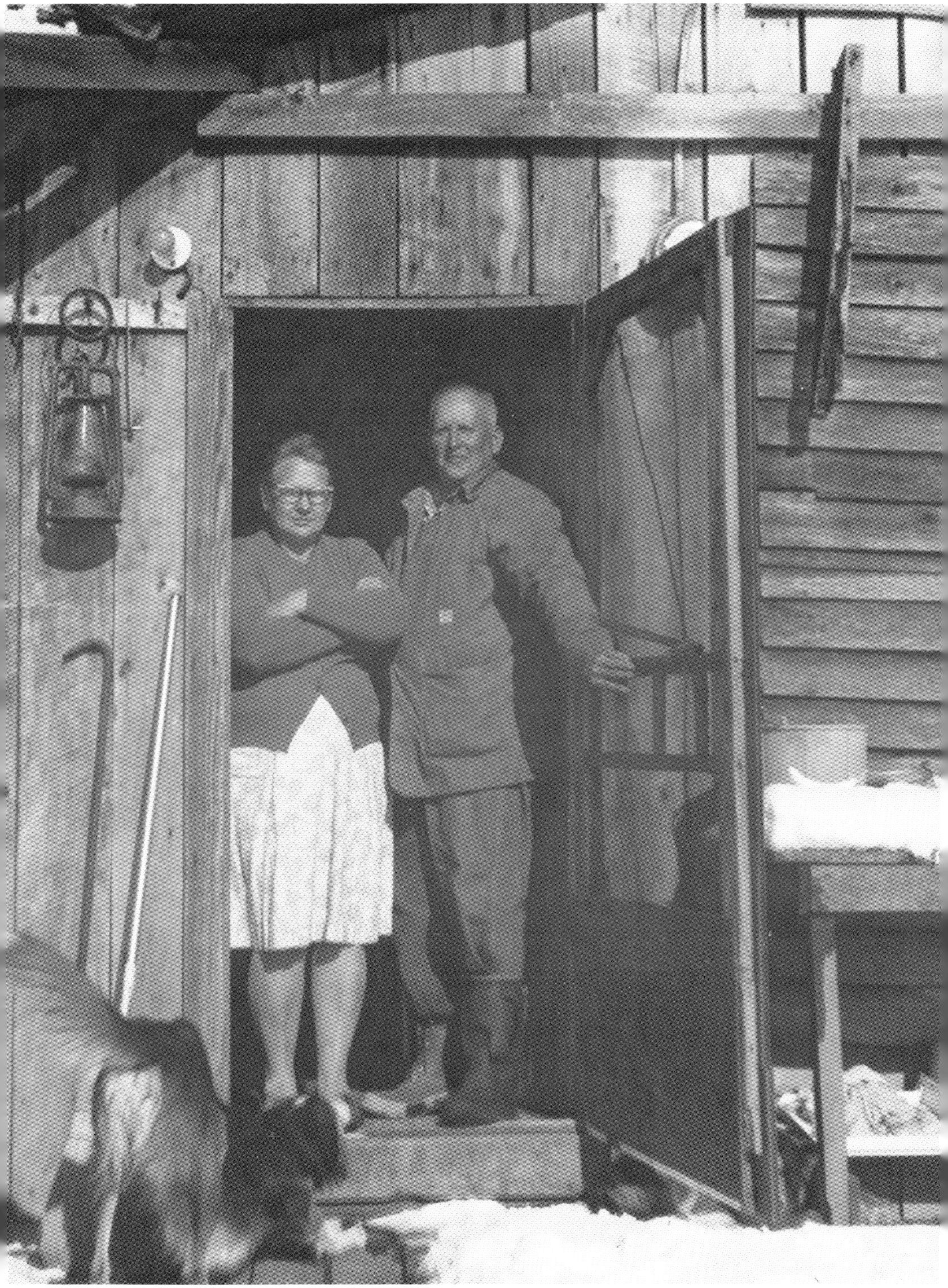

Autumn

I shall give you a new heart, and put a new spirit in you; I shall remove the heart of stone from your bodies and give you a heart of flesh instead.

Ezekiel 36:26

The house was in good shape after 170 years: hand-hewed poplars that surely took a stout yoke of oxen to drag; a rock chimney still in place; rafters straight and true. All but the stairs. They seemed so out of place. They were added on, and were ready to fall down. In some ways the house was like us: the structure, basically sound; the additions, about to collapse. We start with warm fleshy hearts and put stones in their place. Why can't we leave well enough alone?

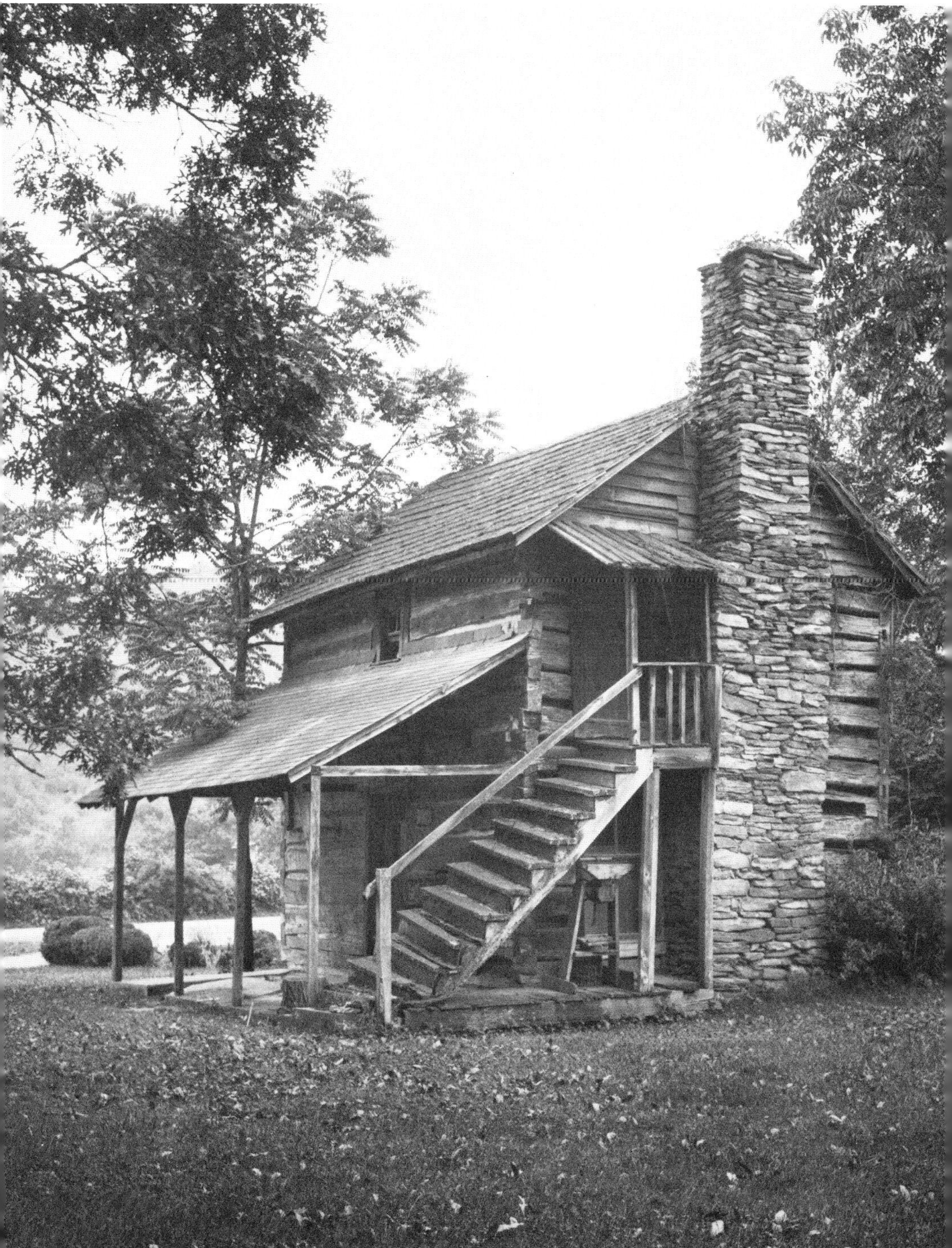

Autumn

*Rest in God alone, my soul!
He is the source of my hope; . . .*
                Psalm 62:5

      Every season has its character. The time is now. The place is where we make it. We can't come to know ourselves in just any spot. Sometimes we have to get away to rest. A million Appalachian coves and inlets and quiet corners invite us to make a nature-filled retreat, to come aside awhile so as to come together again.

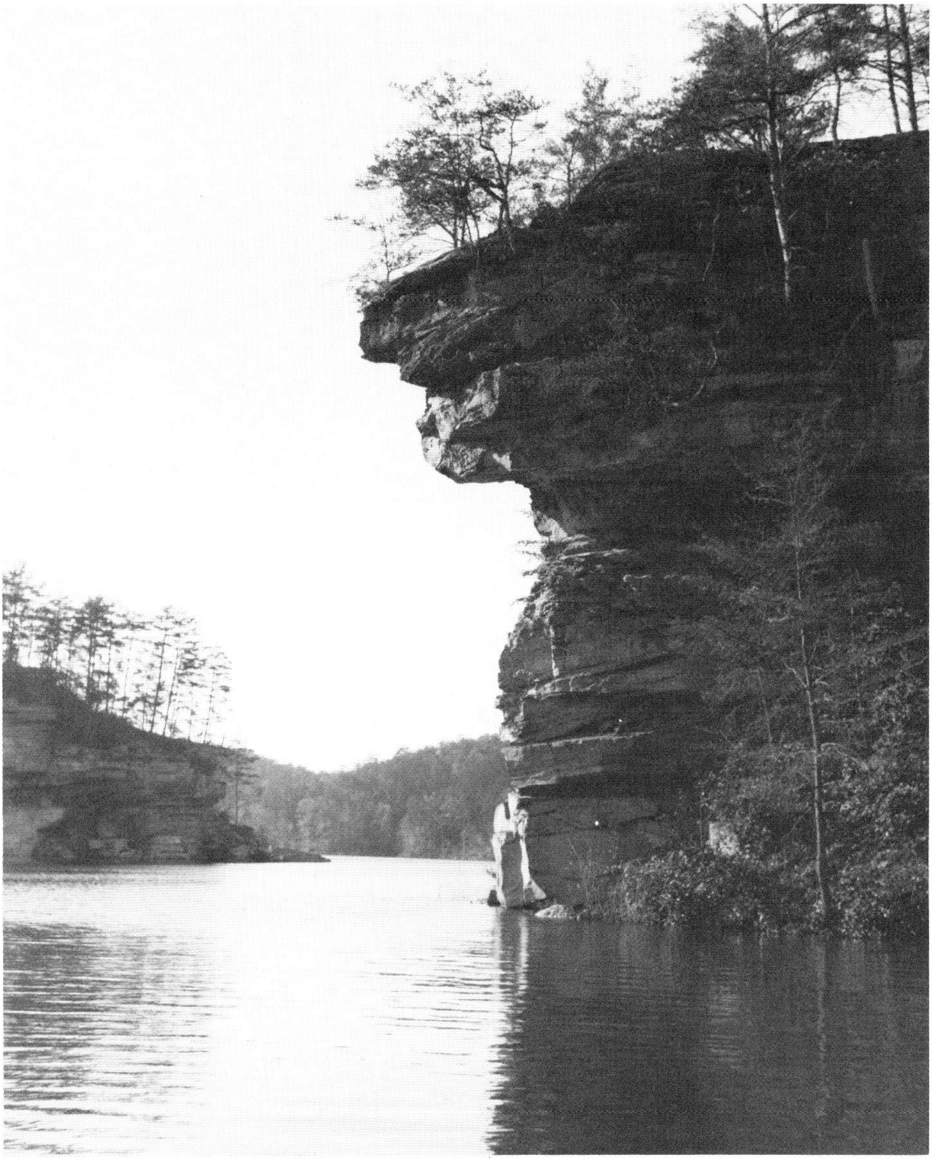

Autumn

*Gathering in summer is the mark of the prudent,
sleeping at harvest is the sign of the shameless.*

Proverbs 10:5

Where should the old ones go? Or should they go at all—to homes for the elderly far away? Why can't they stay put, right here in the heart of things, where they can doze, knit, or just sit. This is their place; they made it so with years of work and worry—but now they want to rest a bit. Don't walk in so fast, and buy your articles, and hustle off. Say a kind word to those who brought us here.

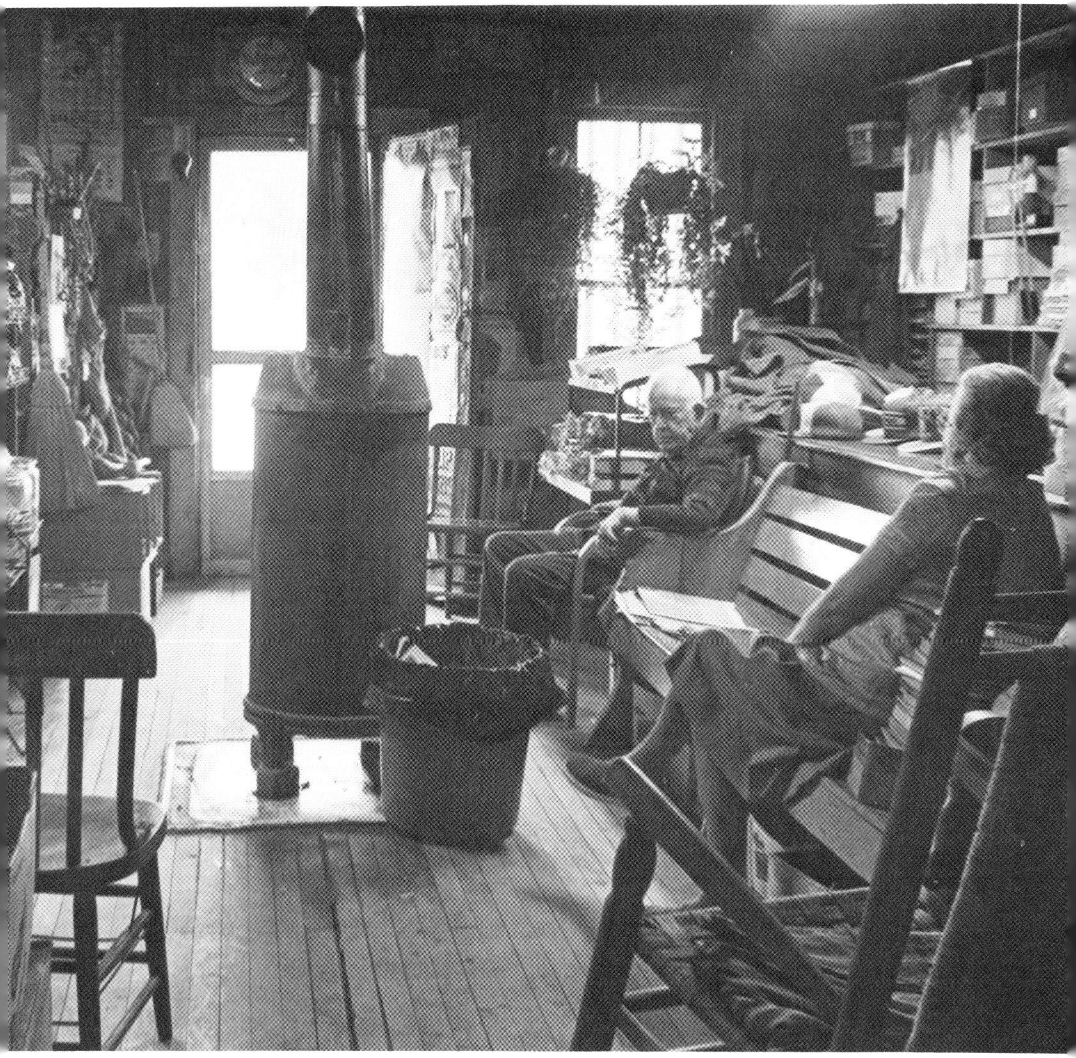

Autumn

> "Land must not be sold in perpetuity, for the land belongs to me, and to me you are only strangers and guests."
>
> Leviticus 25:23

Who really owns these hills? The distant corporation with the mineral rights or timber stands? The wealthy with their "No Trespassing" signs around their summer quarters? The courthouse crowd who know when a piece of land is tax delinquent? The developer who sees not land but dollars? The one who owns a sliver of land on a flood plain with no place to build a safe home? If our answer is "none of these," then there has to be a new approach to land itself. The Indians told us this long ago. So did the Scriptures. Are we so slow to learn?

Autumn

*The sparrow has found its home at last,
the swallow a nest for its young . . .*
                              Psalm 84:3

      Straw stacks and haylofts, thickets and wooded alcoves. Each is a protection, a haven from the elements. In a cool fall nothing was better for a kid than to burrow into a straw stack and feel warm. That's how the birds must feel when they decide to stay here in the hills during the winter.

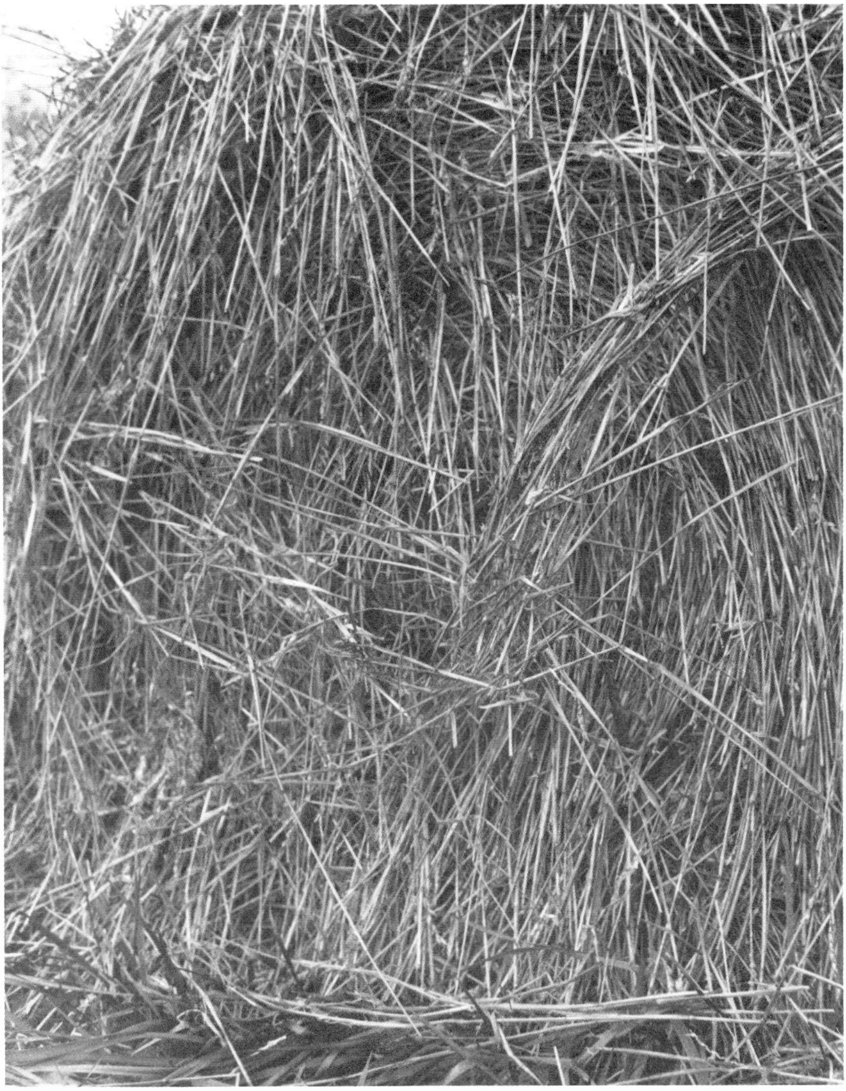

Autumn

Quick to satisfy every need,
  you feed them all with a generous hand.

Psalm 145:16

We rest in thankfulness for the good things of the earth. The tools stop, the corn shocks line up like sentinels before the winter onslaught. The very shadows seem motionless in Indian Summer's glory. A stillness precedes the icy blast. And in this moment's rest all creation gives thanks to God.

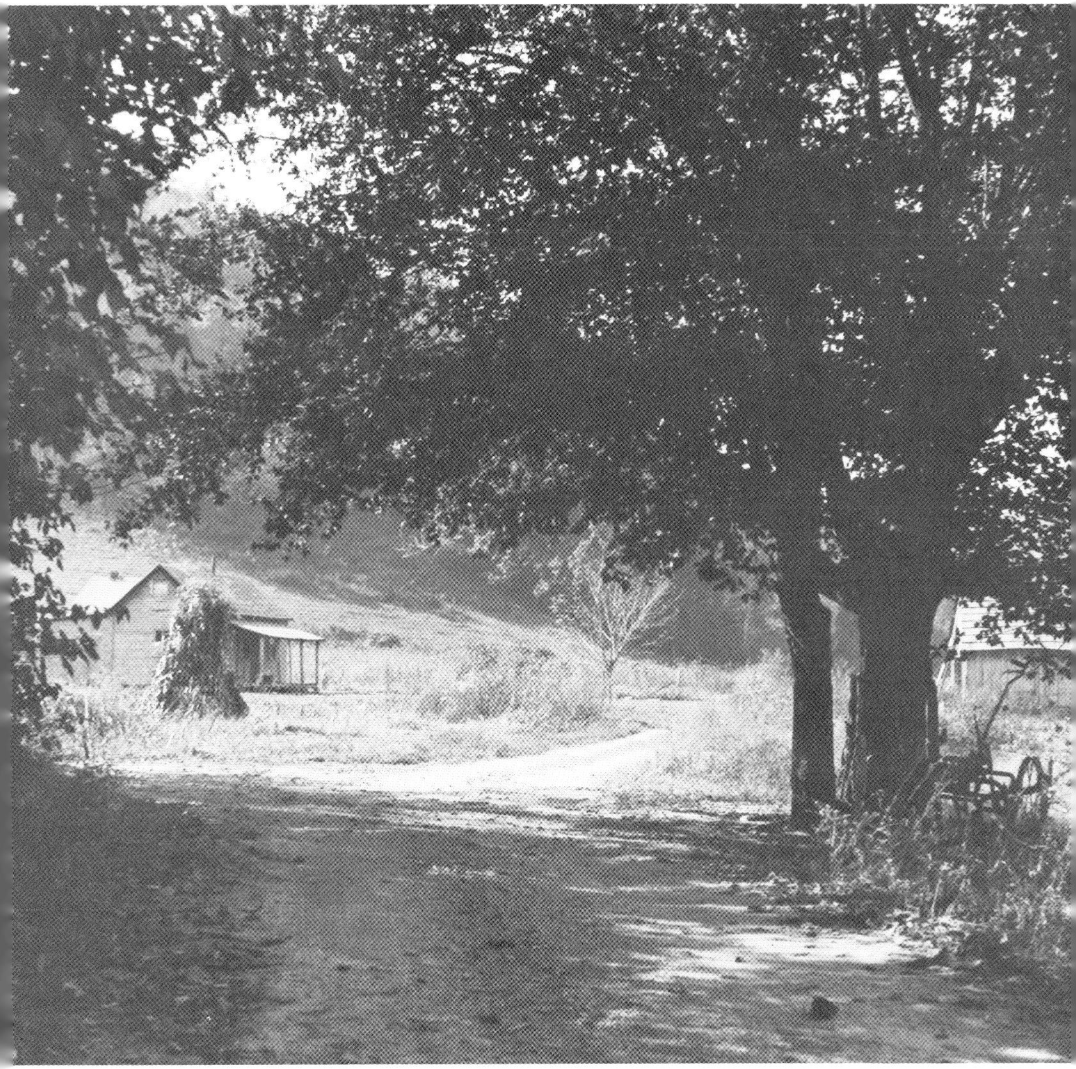

Autumn

*And you will draw water joyfully
from the springs of salvation.*
Isaiah 12:3

They built their homes near the springs. Water determined the location. And it did more. It refreshed and cleaned; it held in the heat and kept out the frost. Water was and is life. We need it to survive. It is our sacrament, our passover, our ebbing forth. We need it pure; and yet the gift of clean water is becoming harder to find. If through water we are saved, then we must save the water.

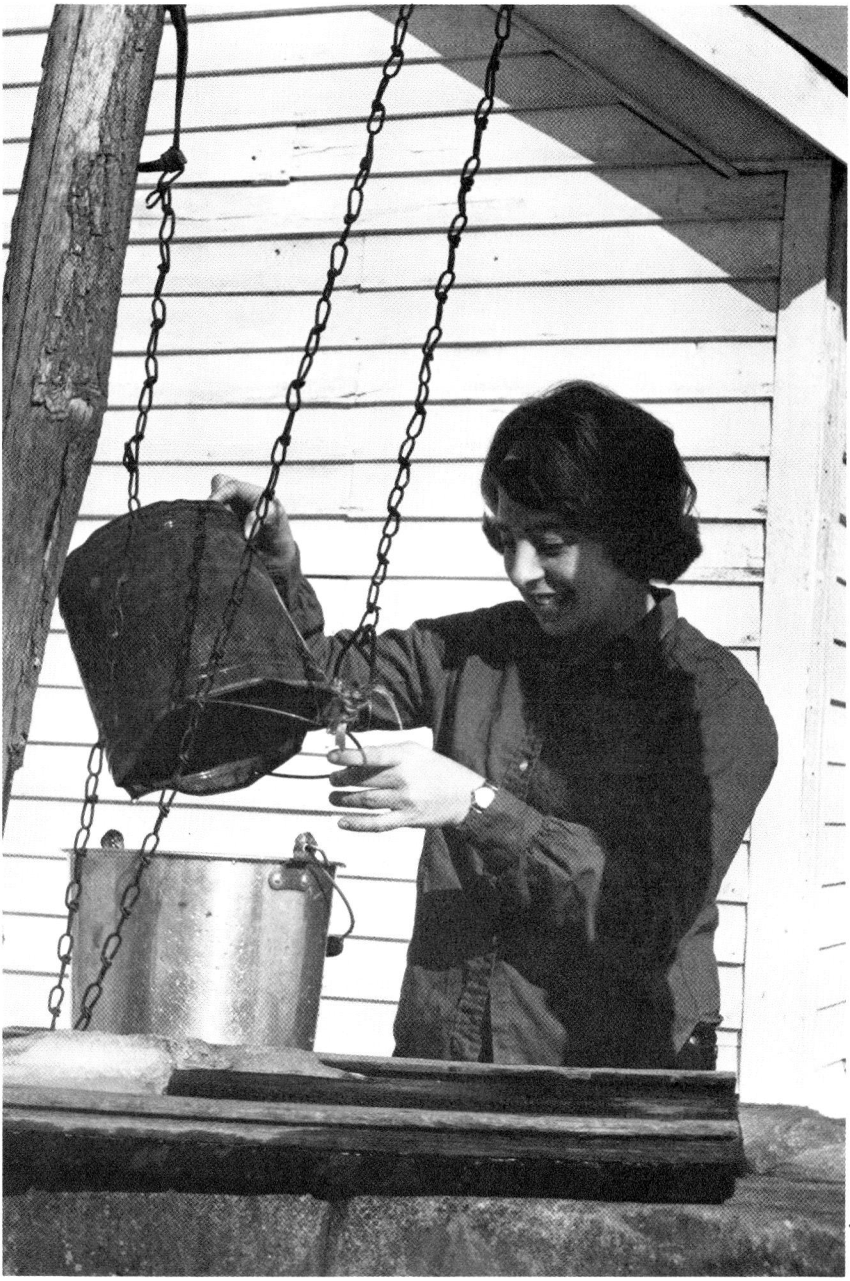

Autumn

*But let justice flow like water,
and integrity like an unfailing stream.*

Amos 5:24

    We call people "just" who give others and themselves their due. They respect all of God's creation; they know how to keep the environment clean, how to make sure the rivers are unpolluted so that fish abound. The just person takes the time to fish and the time to bring others along.

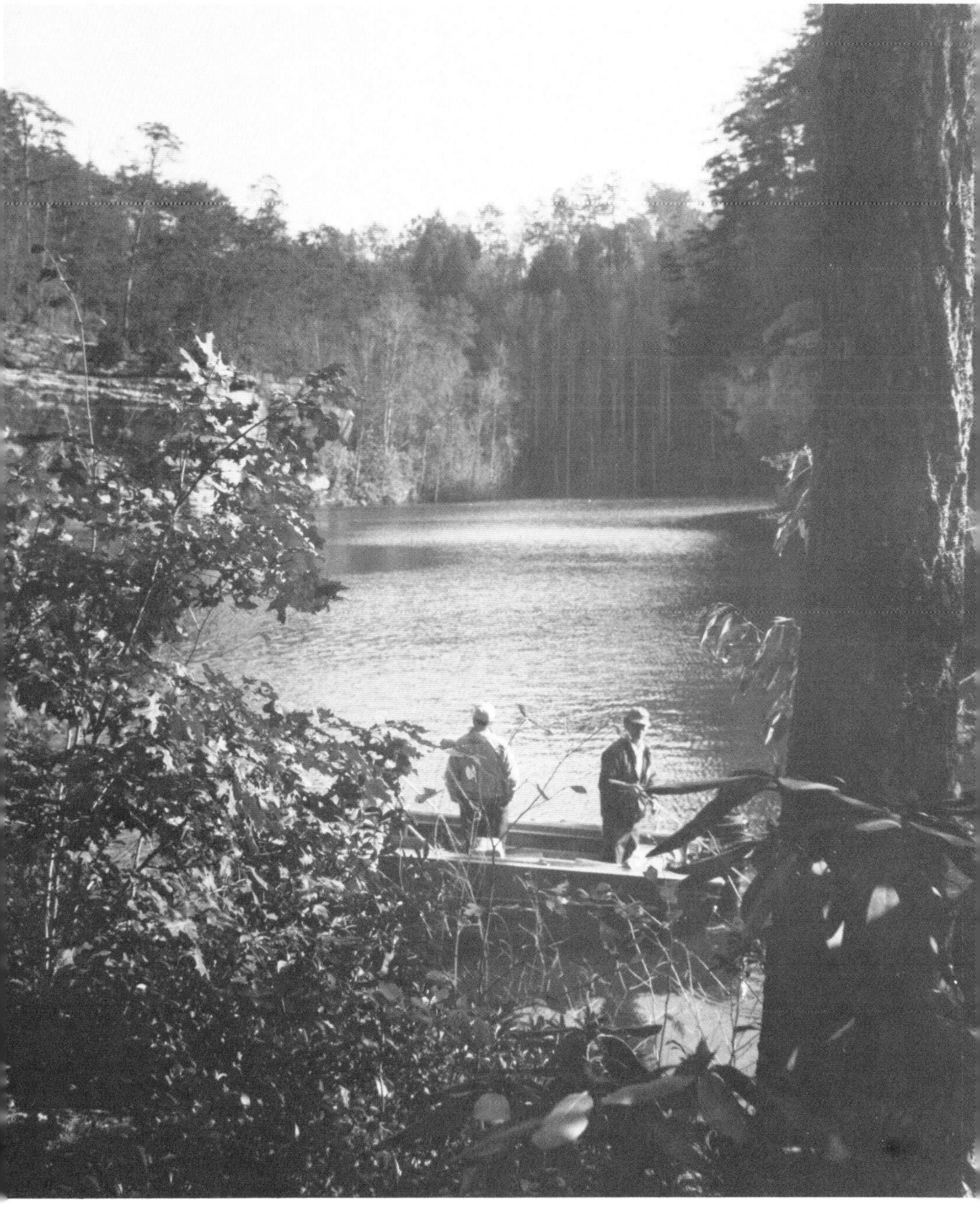

Autumn

*What we are waiting for is what he promised:
the new heavens and new earth, the place where righteousness will be at home.*

2 Peter 3:13

   Are we at home in Appalachia? While there is any injustice in the land, we are not as rooted as we'd like to be. Let this region be the place from which we spring, where we are situated, and where we'll return to the earth. And let all justice reside here.

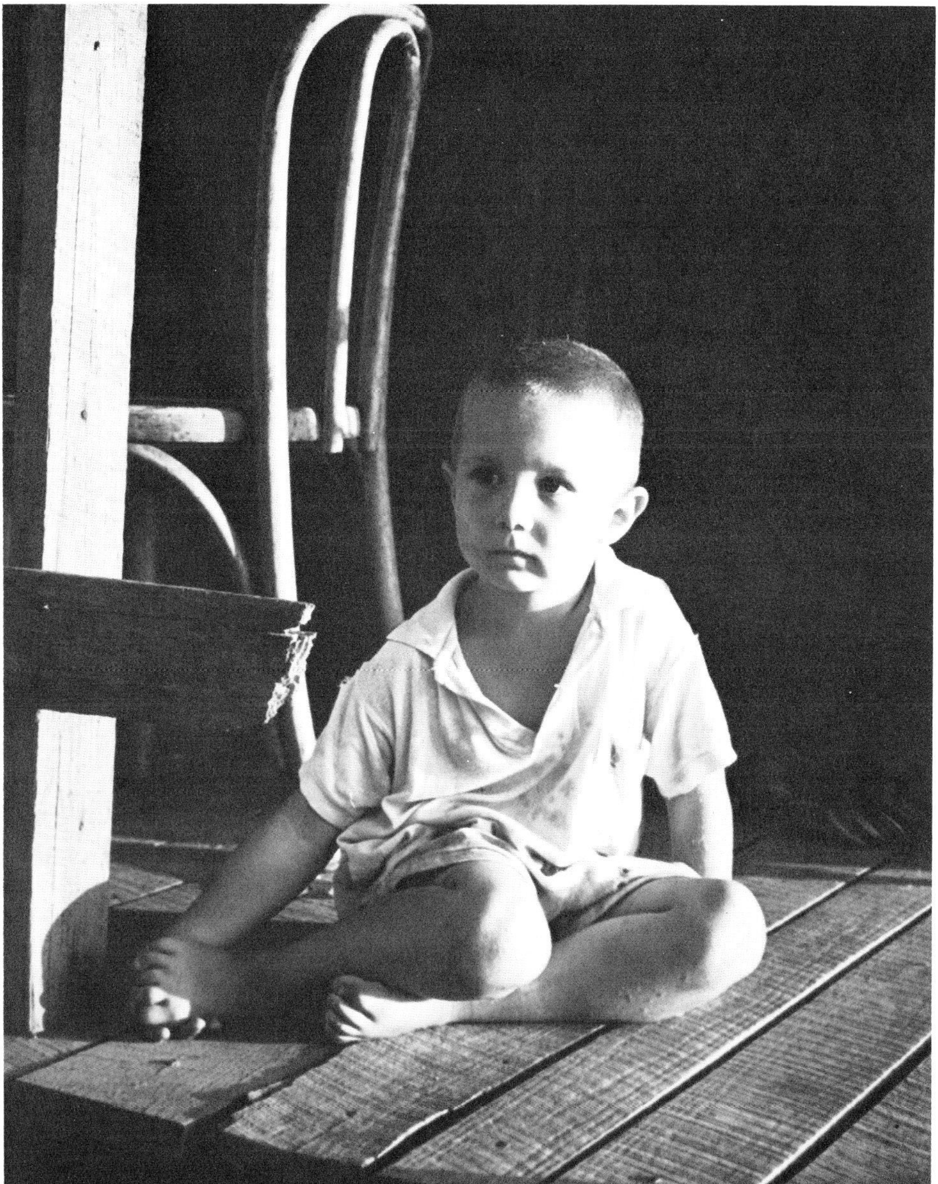